# Praise for
## *Sales Eats First*

"Noel Capon and Gary Tubridy have for the past decade been leading voices in matters related to sales force effectiveness. *Sales Eats First* serves as a blueprint for how to transform a sales organization into a strategic driver of growth and profitability."

*Bruce Dahlgren, Senior Vice President, Hewlett-Packard,*
*Imaging and Printing Group*

"*Sales Eats First* reminds us that the sales force is the voice of the customer. Capon and Tubridy make a compelling argument that companies that keep sales people and sales thinking at their center outperform those that relegate sales to a subordinate role."

*Robert A. Essner, former Chairman and CEO, Wyeth*

"Capon and Tubridy have distilled how the magic of sales excellence is in mastering the fundamentals. As much as we advance the science of sales, it is thoughtful, clear leadership that produces top sales performance. Any business function, internally or externally focused, would benefit from considering how to enable sales to eat first."

*Bill LePage, Senior Vice President, Global Sales Operations, Cisco*

"From the evocative title to the bottom line on sales primacy, *Sales Eats First* drives deeply from the customer — innovation — sales axis. Capon and Tubridy skillfully illustrate how an informed and persevering focus on the customer is at the heart of lucid growth strategy. The authors' rare insight shows us that the pre-recession sales rep has been replaced by a more complex and deeply-embedded sales persona: a thought-leader, a product architect, and a customer advocate."

*Michael Orrick, Senior Vice President, Global Markets Expansion,*
*Thomson Reuters GRC*

"There is no such thing as a great, shrinking company. All corporate success stories have one thing in common — growth! Growth is exciting, boosts corporate morale, increases customer appreciation, drives the stock price, and cures many ills in a company — but no growth occurs without a superior sales culture. *Sales Eats First* illustrates the importance of great leadership and its influence on sales — a must read for anyone who wants to be on a winning team."

*Andy Mattes, Chief Sales Officer (retired), Hewlett-Packard*

"*Sales Eats First* should be essential reading for every salesperson. It shows you how critical it is to pair the art of selling with the science of business. More and more companies are connecting the dots — segmentation, consumer behavior, business behavior, channel management, and supply chain — to achieve organizational sales excellence."

*Mike Fasulo, Executive Vice President, Sony Electronics*

# SALES
# EATS
# FIRST

**How customer-motivated**

**sales organizations**

**out-think, out-offer,**

**and out-perform**

**the competition**

## Also by Noel Capon

*Corporate Strategic Planning*
with John U. Farley and James M. Hulbert

*The Marketing of Financial Services:
A Book of Cases*

*Planning the Development of
Builders, Leaders, and Managers
of 21st Century Business*

*Toward an Integrative Explanation of
Corporate Financial Performance*
with John U. Farley and Scott Hoenig

*The Asian Marketing Case Book*
with Wilfried Van Honacker

#*Marketing Management
in the 21st Century*
with James M. Hulbert
(Chinese edition with Willem Burgers)

*Key Account Management and Planning*
<www.keyaccountmanagement.com>

#*Total Integrated Marketing*
with James M. Hulbert and Nigel E. Piercy

#*The Marketing Mavens*

*\*Managing Global Accounts*
with Dave Potter and Fred Schindler

\*†@*Managing Marketing
in the 21st Century*
with James M. Hulbert

\*†*The Virgin Marketer*

\*†*Capon's Marketing Framework*

\**Strategic Account Strategy*

\*#*Marketing for China's Managers:
Current and Future*
with Willem Burgers and Yuhuang Zheng

\*available at www.axcesscapon.com

\# also published in Chinese

† also published in Spanish

@ also published in Russian

## Also by Gary S. Tubridy

*\*Growth in 2011: A Tale of Two Cities*

*How Companies Use Their Sales Force to
Outmaneuver the Competition
in a Slow Growth Economy*

*\*Advancing the Art of
Customer Motivated Selling*

*\*Sales Leadership Imperatives
in a Tough Economy*

*\*Making the Most out of an
Indifferent Economy*

*\*Sales Force Renewal*

*\*Tough Times Call For Creative Action*

*\*Sales Leadership in Challenging Times*

*Imperatives of Breakthrough
Sales Leadership*

*\*Sales and Marketing:
Collaborating To Grow*

*Sales Force Multipliers – Approaches to
Extending Sales Reach and Impact*

*Mobilizing for Sales Growth:
Sales Operations to the Rescue*

*\*From Transaction to Solution Selling*
with Noel Capon

*\*Increase Sales Yield by Optimizing
Investment in Sales Resource*
with Marc Metzner

\*available at www.alexandergroup.com

# SALES
# EATS
# FIRST

**How customer-motivated**

**sales organizations**

**out-think, out-offer,**

**and out-perform**

**the competition**

by

**NOEL CAPON**

and

**GARY S. TUBRIDY**

Library of Congress Cataloging-in-Publication Data

Capon, Noel

Sales Eats First / Noel Capon and Gary S. Tubridy

p. cm.

ISBN: 978-0-9833300-2-8


Editor: Hilary Hinzmann

Copy Editor: Bonnie Granat

Designer: Anna Botelho

Cover Design: Anna Botelho

# Dedications

To Meyer Feldberg, former Dean of
Columbia Business School,
for his far-sightedness in supporting
the Chief Sales Executive Forum
(www.salesforums.com).
The Chief Sales Executive Forum
formed the critical underpinning for
researching and writing *Sales Eats First*


To James (Mac) Hulbert and
the late W.K. (Bill) Brandt who
provided me with the initial
opportunity to delve deeply
into sales management issues

*Noel Capon*


To my colleagues at
The Alexander Group, especially
Dave Cichelli and Bob Conti,
whose insight and support
made this book possible

*Gary S. Tubridy*

# Acknowledgements

We should like to acknowledge the executives we interviewed who graciously gave of their time and wisdom to make this book possible. They are: Sam Abdelnour — Whirlpool; Wendy Bahr — Cisco; Keith Block — Oracle; Ron Boire — Toys "R" Us; Joe Brennan — Genzyme; Jay Connor — Hewlett-Packard; Bruce Dahlgren — Hewlett-Packard; Dave Edmonds — FedEx; Mike Fasulo — Sony Electronics; James Firestone — Xerox; Gary Flood — MasterCard; Rob Fruithandler — Pitney Bowes; Valarie Gelb — MasterCard; Olivier Kohler — Hewlett-Packard; Rob Lloyd — Cisco; Gregory Lorden — Business Objects; Michael MacDonald — Xerox; Kevin Madden — Honeywell; Jeff Marshall — Pitney Bowes; Andy Mattes — Hewlett-Packard; Kim Metcalf-Kupres — Johnson Controls; Matt Mills — Oracle; George O'Meara — Cisco; Michael Orrick — Thomson Reuters; Sue Petrella — Johnson & Johnson; David Provost — Whirlpool; Daniel Regan — Genzyme; Thomas Schmitt — FedEx; David Smith — Vistakon; Ken Stevens — Sony Electronics; Jay Vandenbree — Sony Electronics; Kevin Warren — Xerox. (For titles, see Appendix 1.)

# Contents

# INTRODUCTION
## Why Sales Eats First —
## And If It Doesn't, Why It Should

**STRICTLY COIN-OPERATED.** Smile as fake as it is broad. A corrupt Willy Loman–*Glengarry Glen Ross* monster whose main product is snake oil. A necessary evil at best.

That's the sales person in the popular imagination and even in some traditional business thinking: Low employee on the totem pole and distant last choice for promotion into general management behind the brainiacs in other functions.

If this stereotype were ever true of the people in consistently successful sales organizations — and we doubt it — it is now completely obsolete, especially in the B2B world that is this book's focus.

Nothing happens until a sale is made. The product never leaves the computer-aided drawing board, the financing never occurs, the service is never provided, the just-in-time supply chain never connects the dots, and no one gets a paycheck until salespeople successfully execute their responsibilities as the interface between their companies and their customers. But the salesperson's job is more than that.

Charged with designing and delivering complex product and/or service solutions that affect every aspect of a customer's operations — and thus responsible for reaching back into every aspect of their own firm's operations (from finance to marketing to new product development) — the modern B2B sales organization must develop and deploy major intellectual capital. Today's top sales organizations courageously venture into areas of complexity and risk, and then inject their intellectual capital into the value propositions that benefit both their customers and their own companies.

Because it bears primary responsibility for customer relationships, the sales organization must also be the guardian of a company's moral compass. It falls first and foremost to salespeople to ensure that an enterprise satisfies customer needs and wants in an ethical manner.

Look at today's most admired and emulated corporations and you see these facts written large in their leadership. In more and more such companies, a rotation into sales, and substantial achievement there, is a requirement for anyone on a path to become a general manager. And executive committees, C-suites, and corporate boards are increasingly peopled by executives who spent significant portions of their careers in sales. They include, among others, John Schwarz, CEO of Business Objects when it was acquired by SAP and now a member of SAP's global executive board; John Chambers, chairman and CEO of Cisco; Henri Termeer, president, chairman, and CEO of Genzyme; Mark Hurd, co-president of Oracle and former president, chairman, and CEO of Hewlett-Packard; William C. Weldon, chairman and CEO of Johnson & Johnson; and Jeff M. Fettig, chairman and CEO of Whirlpool Corporation.

Top leadership roles for ex-salespeople suggest that the popular view of salespeople no longer holds sway. To the contrary, they proclaim the rise of a truly customer-motivated business model.

There's no doubt about it: The most successful companies today are customer-motivated organizations in which sales has the recognized responsibility for identifying customer needs and for crafting and delivering solutions to meet those needs as an equal partner with marketing, product development, and other functions.

This evolution isn't just a passing business fad. Probe the history, current operations, and future planning of companies that are consistent leaders in their industries and you find they have long recognized sales as a key function requiring intellectual and ethical capital on a par with that in every other business area.

That's what this book is about. We have surveyed B2B organizations with complex products, services, and sales processes (it may surprise you to see that our sample includes "old-fashioned" industries such as household appliances as well as "future forward" industries such as information technology and biotechnology) and afterwards asked ourselves the following questions:

- Who are the consistent winners through economic booms and busts? Which companies lead their industries and set the benchmarks that the also-rans try to emulate?

- Who reliably combines organic compound annual growth with dollar volume revenue growth and profitability?

- Most important, what organizational, cultural, and operational characteristics do these companies have in common?

Numbers in hand, we went to talk to senior sales executives at leading corporations. Through generous, in-depth interviews, these executives gave the numbers their essential human and business context. We then performed additional quantitative and qualitative research, including analysis of continuing market share, revenue and profitability numbers, and follow-up interviews. The result was a set of company examples and sales lessons — from Cisco, FedEx, Genzyme, Hewlett-Packard, Honeywell, Johnson & Johnson/Vistakon, Johnson Controls, MasterCard, Oracle, Pitney Bowes, SAP Business Objects, Sony Electronics, Thomson Reuters Legal, Whirlpool, and Xerox — that we believe will stand the test of time.

These firms all excel at the operational nuts and bolts of sales, such as hiring and developing good talent, aligning compensation and performance measures, segmenting customer groups, managing key accounts, and allocating resources across different sales channels. We've mined their experiences for the best of the best in all these areas.

But there's more to how they succeed year in and year out. Different as they are in the flavor and tone of their approaches — just compare, below, how executives from J&J and Oracle talk about their organizations — the top-performing companies share higher-level principles and attributes. These principles and attributes — the soul, heart, character, and intellect of the sales organization — are the real difference makers, the critical components that drive successful operating decisions and initiatives.

The sales organizations of truly customer-motivated companies excel in five areas. They:

- **Lead from the front.** They ensure that all echelons of sales management, from field office to headquarters staff, lead by example in order to coach, mentor, and sell.

- **Speak clearly — and carry a big carrot.** They serve shareholders best by first serving customers, employees, and communities. With regard to what one sales executive described as "the care and feeding of your people," elite sales organizations epitomize the ideal of tough love. They develop and empower their sales forces precisely so that they can then demand the highest levels of achievement from them.

- **Advance the science of sales and the art of the customer relationship.** They rigorously hone and expand their intellectual capital, taking a scientific approach to sales without losing sight of the time-honored art of customer relationships. They combine the best of the old with the best of the new.

- **Make loud mistakes.** Great sales organizations are change friendly. They regularly experiment to refine existing methods and innovate new ones. To that end, they tolerate and even encourage "loud mistakes," experiments conducted in an atmosphere of transparency so that the organization can quickly identify and leverage the learning implicit in the results — good, bad, or indifferent. They understand that their people must have "the freedom to fail," as more than one sales leader put it, if they are to succeed in the long term. They regularly question their business model assumptions and never get complacent. They simultaneously strive for continuous improvement and game-changing plays.

- **Live the mission.** Great sales organizations have a larger mission, and it is no exaggeration to call it a noble purpose, beyond their own revenue and profit goals. As the interface between a firm and its customers, a sales organization must serve as the chief guardian of the firm's ethics and the firm's ultimate purpose in serving customers. Financial rewards naturally drive sales organizations and their people, as they do all of business. But executives across a range of industries and firms agreed that great salespeople are not exclusively "coin operated" and must also be inspired and motivated by a larger mission. The importance of inspiration and motivation applies even to companies known as the toughest, hardest-nosed players in their industries.

We address these five areas of sales excellence in individual chapters. The most important connecting element is the increasing amount of intellectual capital they require. In order to track this theme through a variety of sales processes and systems, especially with regard to sales operations support structures, we have devoted two chapters to advancing the science of sales and the art of the customer relationship. But you will find examples of high-performing sales organizations leveraging intellectual capital in all five areas of sales excellence; quite naturally, these have considerable overlap and connection.

In daily practice, one set of activities usually addresses and reflects multiple sales issues. For example, a sales leader's responsibility to teach and mentor others naturally comes up when we consider leadership as a distinct issue (chapter 1, "Lead from the Front"), when we discuss hiring and training (chapter 2, "Speak Clearly — and Carry a Big Carrot"), and elsewhere. Although we address the five areas — a better word might be aspects — of sales excellence in separate chapters for clarity's sake, we draw frequent explicit connections between them, and they are all implicitly related to one another. Sustaining sales excellence is a holistic activity. The sales organizations we highlight in a particular chapter do not excel only in that single area: They perform at a consistently high level across the board, and we made innumerable close judgment calls in deciding which sales organizations to discuss in each chapter.

Through excellence in all five areas, great sales organizations defeat commoditization in a global economy of over-supply and under-demand in virtually every industrial sector. They show an irrepressible flair for differentiating products in categories where competitors have resigned themselves to believing that differentiation is impossible.

In a nutshell, the extraordinary performance of the organizations cited in this book is rooted in their ability to both enable and inspire their salespeople. You cannot expect your sellers to be the difference-makers between winning and losing if you don't have:

- Leadership that inspires through example.

- Management that articulates clear expectations and helps those who help themselves.

- Infrastructure that captures intellectual capital and enables value-based relationships.

- Innovation from the bottom up and the guts to accept mistakes in the interest of discovering the next big idea.

- A mission larger than the next paycheck that inspires sellers in a way that bonuses and commissions alone simply cannot.

These are the attributes that attract, inspire, enable, and retain the kind of sellers who separate the great organizations from the "also-rans." By paying attention to excellence in all five areas, these companies built customer-motivated sales machines that deliver the numbers, keep the competition at bay, and — unlike products and programs — are very difficult to replicate. Quite simply, customer-motivated sales organizations constitute a huge competitive advantage.

In this book you will find no one-size-fits-all organizational blueprints, selling approaches, or strategies "guaranteed" to produce growth. What you will find are the attributes that great sales organizations and their leaders have in common.

The companies in this book know that customer satisfaction and loyalty are driven by great sales organizations as much as, or more than, they are driven by the products and services a company offers. They know that sales is the linchpin between marketing's understanding of customer needs and finance's understanding of the profit equation. They are pioneering a new *sales-added-value* model that increasingly makes the difference between the best and the rest.

As a result, these companies' sales organizations earn a seat at the table for business-wide decision making. Just as sales has become a more frequent career path for CEOs, so top-performing companies exploit their sales organizations' insight into customer needs to benefit marketing, research and development, and internal processes alike.

One more attribute deserves special mention: The relationship between sales and marketing in customer-motivated firms. The traditional business hierarchy positions marketing as the brains and sales as the brawn. According to this view, the marketing organization sets strategy, segments customers, and designs offers. The sales organization simply executes the instructions it receives from marketing.

High-performing, customer-motivated companies don't operate that way. Instead, sales and marketing are equal partners. They work together as co-architects of strategy, segmentation, and customer offers.

To be sure, sales and marketing still have unique roles to play. Marketing provides a top-down, bird's-eye view of opportunities and challenges, whereas sales provides a bottom-up view of customer needs and solutions. There is an inevitable push and pull between these perspectives. Great companies make that a healthy dynamic and strive for what several senior executives described as "cross-pollination" of sales and marketing.

In the high-performing corporations we discuss, the conventional rigid hierarchy of marketing over sales has given way to a much more fluid relationship in which sales or marketing may take the lead according to changing circumstances. Customer needs and competitive pressures dictate a close, mutually respectful alignment of sales and marketing and shared responsibility for both strategy and execution.

* * *

In the chapters that follow, you'll see the shared principles and attributes of great sales organizations brought to life in varied circumstances, from maintaining and extending dominant market share to developing new markets, adopting new business and sales models, and even leading a turnaround.

Sometimes the whole economy needs a turnaround. The economic crisis that emerged in 2007 and persisted through 2009, threatening companies, investors, and communities around the world, in many ways revealed business at its worst. Driven by a frenzied rush for short-term profits, the subprime mortgage and derivatives markets operated with unthinking disregard for the long-term needs of customers, rank-and-file employees, and communities. In hindsight it was inevitable that the house of cards would sooner or later come crashing down around us.

The companies we highlight show business at its best, putting customers, employees, and communities first. It is no coincidence, in our view, that these companies consistently rank among the most powerful and profitable enterprises in their industries. It is also no coincidence that these companies have come through the downturn in significantly better shape than their competitors.

We believe that understanding the pivotal role that sales organizations play in these leading corporations will benefit anyone in sales, from field and telesales reps to middle managers and senior sales leaders. This book should also be invaluable for those in other functions, especially those that interface with sales. Company-wide management, not least of all CEOs, should also benefit as they learn how to leverage sales excellence to achieve superior business performance.

Likewise, investors who want to identify the best risk–reward scenarios would be well advised to target companies with high-performing sales organizations. There is likely no better barometer of company health and prospective value.

Finally, for those who mistakenly believe that business can never look beyond short-term goals, the companies and practices we discuss prove that it just isn't so.

Before we delve into the content, a word about the book's title. One of our chapters highlights the successful transformation of a struggling core business unit in a global conglomerate. The transformation only gained momentum when the head of the business unit decreed, "Sales eats first." These words encapsulate everything that we've just sketched out, and that the rest of the book will explore in detail, about the stature, responsibilities, and challenges of the 21st century sales organization. If sales doesn't eat first in your company, you'd better ask why not and begin working to change the situation. It's the best recipe for sustainable success you can find.

Now let's look at how great sales organizations combine world-class practices in strategy, organizational structure, and performance management to out-think, out-offer, and out-sell the competition.

# CHAPTER 1
# Lead from the Front

**"PORSCHE. THERE IS NO SUBSTITUTE."** Maybe you recall Tom Cruise repeating that iconic advertising slogan in the movie *Risky Business*. Well, all the evidence we know says loud and clear: "Sales leadership. There is no substitute."

Outstanding sales organization performance begins with outstanding sales leadership. Trying to function without it puts your whole business at risk. In terms of the intellectual capital that today's sales organizations must acquire and deploy, great leadership is like seed money. It's the initial investment that sets the direction. In this chapter we explore how the leaders of great sales organizations:

- Spend lots of time in the field to observe, inspect, teach, coach, and sell.

- Lead by example and in collaboration with the sales force and cross-functional colleagues.

- Develop leadership throughout the organization and ensure effective hand-offs between leaders at all levels, from front-line sales managers to senior executives.

- Build great teamwork.

- Foster "acting like it's your own business," empowering salespeople to take initiative in crafting and delivering customer value.

- Lead by listening, developing business and market insight that gives meaning to the numbers by engaging both the sales organization and customers in two-way communication.

- Are the first to enter areas of market risk and complexity to innovate new ways of delivering customer value and spearhead sales model and organizational change.

\*\*\*

1

# *Spend Lots of Time in the Field*

Despite differences in rhetorical style and areas of emphasis, the executives we spoke to all agreed that sales leaders must regularly get out from behind their desks to work in the field with sales representatives and customers. Keith Block, executive vice president of Oracle North America,[1] memorably summed up this aspect of organizational sales excellence as "leading from the front:"

> *There are some fundamental principles to sales excellence: The right products and services, the right sales model and strategies, the right talent, the right incentives, the right behavior, and the right culture. At the core of that is the right leadership.*
>
> *You can either lead from the front or you can lead from the back. Our people lead from the front.*

Digging into the issue, we found that sales organizations perform best when their leaders, from headquarters executives to local sales managers, lead by example and in collaboration with rank-and-file salespeople. Leading by example and collaboration does not imply any confusion about who is in charge or where the buck stops. Tough orders must still be given and followed. But the necessity to lead by example and in collaboration with others reflects the intellectual capital that today's elite sales organizations must deploy to outperform the competition.

Especially in the B2B world, sales reps must increasingly be able to take the lead in identifying and coordinating complex sets of resources so as to craft value propositions for customers. These propositions must deliver value to both their customers and their own companies. Resources include the wisdom, internal clout, and high-level customer relationships of senior sales executives; the expertise of specialist sales and cross-functional colleagues; and diverse product and service sets.

Leading by example and in collaboration with others crucially extends to relationships with customers. The direct input and feedback of customers may not only help tailor solution packages but may also play an important role in the firm's new product development.

Most important of all, leading from the front defines how the most successful sales organizations venture into areas of complexity and risk and thereby transform markets by creating new ways of serving customer needs.

---

1 All interviewee's organizational positions noted as at the time of the most recent interview.

Regarding product development and customization as well as penetrating new markets, sales organization heads can commit their firms to individual customers and market segments in ways salespeople and other executives cannot. This ability constitutes one of the main reasons that top sales executives should lead from the front. At the same time, they must empower those below them in the organization to take the initiative and commit appropriate resources so as to craft and deliver customer value. Empowerment, too, requires that sales leaders get into the field to encourage, coach, and support the desired behavior.

It was fascinating to learn from sales leaders at Oracle and other top companies both how they lead from the front and how they foster that behavior throughout their organizations. The lessons we draw from their experiences cross all industries and all organizational cultures, from the most rough-and-tumble to the most supportive and nurturing.

## *Lead by Example*

Think that Oracle has a buccaneering, piratical, ruthless, exclusively "coin-operated" sales organization with little regard for customers?

Think again.

An extraordinary change within the Oracle sales organization has made that opinion obsolete. In recent years, the business press has been full of stories on Oracle's growth by acquisition. But Oracle has also achieved consistent impressive organic growth precisely because its sales organization has become world class in creating and delivering customer value before, during, and after the sale.

Keith Block, who runs Oracle's North American sales organization and sits on the firm's executive committee, shared how senior sales management "changed the mind-set" of the sales organization and transformed customer–company relationships by getting into the field to "observe, inspect, teach, coach, and sell." The story has much in common with those of the other high-performing sales organizations we profile, but — and it is no surprise with this famously aggressive, even pugnacious, company — it has a tone and emphasis unique to Oracle.

Showing a willingness to confront mistakes and problems shared by all great companies, Keith Block frankly acknowledged that negative perceptions of Oracle sales practices once had some foundation in truth. Block said,

"Historically, we would produce a product and we would push it out there without a lot of customer input and feedback." The products were good, and "we had fantastic numbers in the 1990s. But ask the customers what they thought of us back then, and the survey results would not be positive. Ask the customers what they think of us now, and it's completely different."

If Oracle had "just gone by the numbers, because everybody was buying our software," Block added, it would have risked sabotaging its continuing success with "slash-and-burn techniques. That guy you just sold is not going to make the same purchase down the road because he's pretty mad at you for doing what I've referred to as 'drive-by selling.'"

The trust and loyalty Oracle has earned from its customers since then began with its sales leadership team. Block observed, "Oracle historically performs best when we set our sights on a rival. It's like a laser focus. SAP is in our cross hairs right now." Although the sales organization continues to "establish a rallying cry" at that level, in recent years it has had an over-arching rallying cry that looks past competitors to customers. When Block took over the top sales leadership role, "the first set of messages that went out were about 'relationship, solutions, service' and establishing long-term relationships with our customers. That continues to be the number-one thing we talk about."

Going from rhetoric to reality required a change in sales force behavior. Block said, "This is where we have transformed so much. It used to be that the two most important aspects of a sales rep at Oracle were 'mercenary' and 'coin-operated.'"

Without in any way slighting the profit motive, because "everybody in sales, everybody in business, has to be coin-operated to a certain extent," Block explained that Oracle had to develop and hire sales representatives "who are customer-focused, who care about the customer, and who are going to work hard to understand the business problems of customers in their industries." There had to be "a transformation from *grow at all costs* to *grow the right way*. And the right way is *not* at the customer's expense."

Such a transformation "can be very disruptive," Block said, "and some-times that's good. In this case I think it was good, because we needed a change in culture." The sales organization had to "bring in new people who had the same values toward what the customer relationship is all about. If you have good leaders, good leaders will bring in other good people, and productive change cascades down the wall."

New blood in the sales organization did not mean wholesale turnover, however. Block emphasized that "even people who are by nature mercenary and coin-operated want to follow a good leader. If you have a great regional sales manager, the sales reps will do anything for him. And if you can make that scalable, you build a great sales organization."

At the same time, it took "constant inspection to change people's mindsets and behavior. You have to watch for bad behavior and weed it out." This requirement applied to the best sales reps as well as lesser performers, because even "great athletes need guidance to focus on the right things."

In turn there needed to be a change in the behavior of Oracle's sales management, from headquarters staff to regional managers. Echoing remarks we heard at other top-performing sales organizations, Block observed that a sales force cannot fulfill a new sales model without good training and coaching. Accordingly, he sought to change the Oracle sales culture from the top down:

> I remember growing up in the organization, and I used to see sales management in the office a lot. You need to get out there. I want the guys out there so they observe and they teach. If you're going to be a leader, you must learn how to teach. Your job is to teach.

> You walk around here now and you're not going to see people. They're not here. They're out there with the sales reps in front of customers, and that's where they need to be.

One of the primary reasons for sales leaders to get out in the field is to assess sales rep performance and productivity. Oracle pays close attention to the sales reps' numbers, does "territory reviews every quarter," and "we inspect, and we inspect, and we inspect." But the numbers alone can be deceiving, as Block explained:

> You can look at a sales rep's numbers and say, "Wow, this guy does double his quota every year. He's fantastic!"

> Well, that doesn't tell the whole story. He may be getting double quota attainment, but he may be really upsetting customers with slash-and-burn techniques.

It is not that quota attainment has become less important at Oracle. Far from it. Keith Block left us in no doubt that the Oracle culture "is a culture of growth. It's highly competitive and demanding. You may have done a great job last quarter. But what are you going to do this quarter? It's that pace, it's that cadence, it's that push."

But the sales organization has become more supportive. Block said, "Historically, if you didn't make your number in a quarter, poof! You were gone! We take a little bit longer-term perspective now. We treat our people better, and I think you have to do that." In short, Oracle "has softened — a little bit. I mean, if somebody is consistently performing poorly quarter after quarter, well, you're either going to be the right guy in the job or you're not going to be the right guy."

Leading from the front and fostering leadership throughout the sales force have also helped drive a change within Oracle from generalist to specialist sales roles. We address the issues of developing great salespeople and determining their roles in a customer-motivated sales model, respectively, in chapter 2, "Speak Clearly — and Carry a Big Carrot," and in chapters 3 and 4, "Advance the Science of Sales and the Art of the Customer Relationship, Part 1" and "Advance the Science of Sales and the Art of the Customer Relationship, Part 2," with reference to a broad range of high-performing sales organizations, including Oracle's.

Here let's note how other top sales organizations share Oracle's focus on leading from the front. For example, Greg Lorden, senior vice president for sales and marketing and general manager of SAP Business Objects, Oracle's nemesis, stressed the need for sales executives to get out in the field "as much as we can, because our job is out there" with customers and sales reps. "Lead by example," he added. "Don't ask anything you wouldn't do or didn't do."

Knowing we were planning a book on sales organization excellence, Lorden urged us to focus on leadership. "What's missing from business books in general," he said, "is the real cycle of leadership and performance. I haven't seen that articulated well." We hope he sees it here, at least as expressed in his and other sales leaders' insights.

The sales executives we spoke to consistently emphasized that good sales habits must "come from the top," as MasterCard's Gary Flood put it. At Honeywell Building Solutions, a successful turnaround effort crucially began with changes in sales leadership and cascaded down through the organization (see chapter 2, "Speak Clearly — and Carry a Big Carrot"). A sales leader at a telecom firm told us that important sales initiatives and sales model changes "only succeed from the top down," because desired field behavior will be stymied by conflicting agendas at different levels of sales management otherwise.

In this context, sales leaders repeatedly mentioned the importance of genuine support and respect for sales in the firm's C-suite, an issue we explore in chapter 7, "Sales-Added Value: The New Model for Great Sales Organizations — and Great Corporations." Executives at Cisco, Genzyme, Whirlpool, and Xerox also pointed specifically to the sales zeal and/or background of their CEOs. Rob Lloyd, executive vice president for worldwide operations at Cisco, said that Cisco CEO John Chambers "thinks like a salesman-in-chief." Joe Brennan and Dan Regan, respective heads of sales of Genzyme Biosurgery and Genzyme Renal, observed that Henri Termeer, the company's CEO for more than 25 years, began working in the health-care industry as a young MBA graduate when he became a sales and marketing manager at Baxter International. Whirlpool's current CEO, Jeff Fettig, and his immediate predecessor, Dave Whitwam, both led the company's sales and marketing efforts before ascending to the top job. And Xerox's remarkable turnaround in the early 2000s, led by then CEO Anne Mulcahy (previously a senior sales executive and by no means the first Xerox sales leader to become Xerox CEO), surely could not have succeeded if the company did not treat sales as a core business function (see chapter 5, "Make Loud Mistakes").

No subject we discussed with sales executives evoked more unanimity than the need to get out in the field and lead by example, to show, in the words of Ken Stevens, senior vice president for national accounts at Sony Electronics, that management and sales reps "all do the same job." One of the most important observations we can share of great sales organizations is that they do not use titles as a surrogate for leadership. They understand that these are not one and the same.

In the most successful sales organizations, senior sales executives are highly visible in the field, as they interact with their own people and with customers. They are the first to test a new presentation or a new positioning. They insist on hearing directly from both sales reps and customers about what is working and what is not.

We confidently say to those in general management as well as sales: If your sales leadership is not willing to go out and see and hear things directly, and then take the necessary steps to improve, you will lose the game.

As we've already heard from Oracle's Keith Block, sales leaders must go into the field to see what lies behind the numbers individual sales reps are producing. As a senior sales executive at a global services firm put it, "You confront the grim realities by tying anecdotes to analytics. You meet with sales reps in every region, you bring back what you learn, you tie it to the analytics, and then you start to make decisions."

In addition to providing business insight, field visits are essential to building morale and team spirit, a subject we discuss in depth in chapter 2, "Speak Clearly — and Carry a Big Carrot." Genzyme's Dan Regan spoke of the need to stay engaged with a sale force on a personal level as it expands along with revenue and profit growth. "When we were 38 people in the Genzyme Renal sales force, I was 'Dan' to everyone," Regan said. Without lots of time in the field, the danger is that "I'll only be 'senior vice president of Genzyme Renal' to too many sales reps."

As in much of business, the "soft" side has a "hard" aspect, and vice versa. Cisco's Rob Lloyd, among other executives at a range of companies, described how personal contact with sales reps and customers makes it possible to identify best practices that should be scaled across a sales organization.

A word about the travel this entails. Genzyme's Joe Brennan told us, "I was on the road 48 weeks last year." This was the highest number we heard, but not by any large order of magnitude. Such constant travel obviously takes a physical toll and can be hard on one's family and personal life.

Cisco's Rob Lloyd asserted, "[Travel is] the best way to open and develop relationships but not the most effective way to maintain them." For that Cisco is turning more and more to what it calls "telepresence" technologies, which it also sees as a growing business line alongside its core network products like routers and switches. Via telepresence facilities in Cisco's briefing centers at company headquarters and around the world, Lloyd and his fellow sales leaders aim "to increase by twofold the percentage of time we spend in customer and sales rep interactions, with less time spent in cramped airplane seats and more time at home with our families."

Many of the high-performing sales organizations we highlight in this book, including Oracle, Hewlett-Packard, and SAP Business Objects, use briefing centers for virtual as well as in-person meetings with customers and field sales reps. Social networking technologies such as those at the heart of Facebook and Twitter are also becoming increasingly important. But it is unlikely that leading from the front can ever be solely or mainly a virtual activity. Cisco's Rob Lloyd told us that he and his peers expect to continue to travel selectively, because it serves so many important business purposes.

Oracle's Keith Block emphasized how forays into the field support his sales organization's main rallying cry of "relationship, solutions, service," which functions as both a guiding principle and a profit driver for sales of everything from "entry-level database licenses" to the most complex technology and applications solutions. Block said, "The sales reps know that [at] every sale, you're solving a customer problem, and you work your way backward from that. If you take that position, you will always work to do what's best for the customer."

Block told us that to sustain and build on that behavior Oracle sales leadership must continue to "lead from the front" and "model character, integrity, and most of all, accountability."

## *Act Like It's Your Own Business*

Keith Block observed that poorly performing sales organizations, like dysfunctional organizations in general, tend to blame outside forces for their failures. "You know how it goes," Block said. "You hear, 'I wasn't successful because of the development organization or the marketing organization or the sales support organization or whoever. It's the other guy's fault.' I can't stand that. If you didn't make the sale, it's because you didn't make it happen. It had nothing to do with the other guy."

Block noted that great products and services alone are not enough to earn customer trust and loyalty in today's competitive markets. We heard similar comments over and over again in our talks with sales executives, who agreed that over the long term the real differentiator is not product or price but the relationship a sales organization builds with the customer (see chapters 3 and 4, "Advance the Science of Sales and the Art of the Customer Relationship, Part 1" and "Advance the Science of Sales and the Art of the Customer Relationship, Part 2"). Likewise, Block explained:

> *As part of the sales organization, you obviously depend on other organizations within Oracle. You depend on marketing to get the right messages out. You have to have a product that's good enough to sell. But that's kind of where it ends, and it becomes the ownership of the sales organization. Because the front-line customer relationship is with you.*

9

Reiterating that sales leaders must model behavior that "cascades down" through the sales organization, Block continued:

> *I can't imagine being a sales leader on any level and not having the mentality that you're the one who's judged, you're the one who's accountable, you own it. So act like it's your own business. If you were running a small shop on the corner, what would you do to survive in tough times?*
>
> *If you have that mentality every day, you're going to make something happen. You almost will it to happen.*

One of the most important aspects of this mentality, Block asserted, is that it drives effective experimentation in sales models, internal processes, and customer relationship management. The need to experiment regularly for the sake of continuous improvement and of transformations to keep pace with — or better yet, anticipate — evolving markets was another point of agreement among the sales leaders we interviewed. We share their views and our related findings in chapter 5, "Make Loud Mistakes."

Block remarked that "act[ing] like it's your own business" means that sales leaders must get into the field not only to observe and coach the sales reps but to also sell. We've already mentioned the widely shared view that good sales habits must "come from the top." Likewise, Hewlett-Packard's Andy Mattes told us, "As you work up the food chain, sales management needs to be in selling mode and call on their peers" in the customer's organization (see chapter 3, "Advance the Science of Sales and the Art of the Customer Relationship, Part 1"). The reason, Keith Block said, is to help overcome customers' risk aversion and raise their comfort level:

> *Customers have become much more risk averse. They buy on value and comfort. I've been around the world this week visiting customers, and C-level executives come into the room and look you in the eye and say, 'Your software can fit our business. But tell us how you're going to make us successful. And how do we know you're not going to disappear after the sale is made?'*
>
> *One of these customers is in a very remote location. It's more likely you'd go to China than to this place. The team did a wonderful job, and they really won the day. But I've been there twice in the last three months to demonstrate our commitment, and our head of applications development has also gone there, so that we could lay*

*out the plan on how we are going to deploy our offer. That makes a huge difference.*

This example illustrates how, in a globalized economy in which customers can almost always choose functionally equivalent products and services from more than one vendor, it is the sales organization that must ultimately create a compelling value proposition. Fostering "act[ing] like it's your own business" and driving leadership initiatives throughout its ranks, from managers to sales reps, is the Oracle sales organization's primary tool for creating compelling customer value. Block declared, "If you sit there and say, 'It's not my job, it's not my responsibility,' then the organization fails, the company fails, customers fail."

All our interviewees stressed the importance of freeing front-line sales managers, in particular, to lead by example and to spend a major portion of their time coaching sales reps, especially by observing them in action on sales calls. They also agreed that sales leaders must also enable, encourage, and indeed require sales reps to show leadership initiative of their own.

The Genzyme sales organization, for example, wants its people to emulate the sales rep who "has grown his territory four times faster than anyone else." Describing how this rep has taken a leadership role among his peers, Joe Brennan said:

> *His big message to the sales force is, "You shouldn't wait for your manager to tell you what you are doing right and not doing right. You have to become a master of your craft."*
>
> *He also tells them, "The process is never done. I still have to make improvements. I have to learn from you, too." And he queries them on what they do and how they are successful.*

At Thomson Reuters Legal, Michael Orrick, general manager and vice president of the information provider's U.S. law firms channel, "coaches and encourages a franchise mentality, where salespeople own ultimate responsibility for optimizing their accounts and owe that accountability to our stockholders and stakeholders." At Sony, Ken Stevens said he tells the sales force the following:

> *Never let a sales budget or headquarters stand in the way of doing good business. Make the case for good business, and we'll find a way to do it.*

*But you have to make the case. You have to put it all together. You have to show the profitability and the return. And if you show us, we'll find a way.*

Chapter 2, "Speak Clearly — and Carry a Big Carrot," looks more closely at the challenge of hiring and training both good front-line sales managers and effective sales reps. Here let's look next at how, as we heard from Keith Block and his counterparts at other top sales organizations, sales leaders must also explicitly share their leadership in a collaborative way with sales reps, colleagues in other functions, and customers.

## *Share the Power*

Cisco's Rob Lloyd told us about his and his colleagues' management style: "We are evolving as a sales organization from command and control to excellence through collaboration." Our sense is that all the sales organizations we highlight in this book could be described in these terms, with some being farther along in the evolutionary process than others.

As we said at the outset of the chapter, however, this evolution does not indicate any real blurring of authority or of the responsibility to make and execute tough decisions. All these companies continue to maintain clear, effective chains of command. But as modern sales roles have evolved, they have become too complex for every move to be regimented from on high. Both individual sellers and teams of salespeople have to respond flexibly and on the fly to customer needs without the sales organization as a whole losing its coherence. Sales leaders must accordingly foster personal initiative in combination with great teamwork throughout their organizations.

One of the most significant changes that Keith Block and his management team have led at Oracle is a shift from generalist to specialist sales roles, abandoning "an account manager model" for one in which "[t]hat person [account manager] doesn't exist anymore. You're either selling applications, technology, or hardware, period, end of story."

Increasing specialization of sales roles marks many, if not all, industries. Sales organizations have responded to this issue in a variety of ways. Some, like Oracle, have aggressively declared the end of the generalist sales rep. Others match a mix of generalists and specialists against accounts of different size and complexity. There is no single common denominator for today's sales organizations on the value of generalists compared to specialists, except that the intellectual capital demands have risen across the board for both generalist and specialist sellers. We explore a variety of successful responses to this challenge in chapter 3, "Advance the Science of Sales and the Art of the Customer Relationship, Part 1." Here we note how Oracle flexibly modified its new approach at large, complex accounts in order to ensure efficient hand-offs between specialist salespeople and to foster leading from the front among all of them.

This topic emerged when we asked Block if there was a problem coordinating multiple sales specialists calling on the same account. His answer was no in most cases, because even if "multiple sales forces are swarming on an account, our CRM sales force is calling on the customer's sales and marketing and call center; our technology sales force is calling on the data center and the CTO; our ERP sales force is calling on the CFO, and so on. So you don't see a lot of collisions."

Yet the presence of multiple salespeople "does create consternation internally for some very large customers who have procurement offices for centralized buying." To deal with this issue, Block said, "If we had six sales reps calling on the account, we picked the one with the best relationship with the customer and said, 'We're anointing you the greater amongst equals. You're the player-coach, and you call the shots.' And that was an informal program, an experiment."

The experiment worked so well that Oracle scaled up the "greater amongst equals" approach as a formal program for large, complex accounts with centralized buying. For these customers there is now "a key account director," a specialist sales rep who receives extra compensation not for being a single point of contact like Oracle's old style generalist account manager, but for fulfilling some of that same function by "coordinating all sales activity and making sure that all the account planning activities are lined up."

Other leading sales organizations have different approaches, but Oracle's solution is a far cry from the role of the traditional generalist account manager. Oracle's player-coaches are not always in the game, or even necessarily in the same arena during important parts of the action. They often hand off full responsibility for selling engagements to their peers rather than always being involved like a traditional account manager. It's also important to catch the fact that Oracle wants its sales reps to practice team-oriented behavior as a matter of course, whether there is or is not a designated key account director.

The flip side of being personally accountable and not blaming others, Block said, is a recognition that everyone must pull together to achieve the sales organization's goals: "It's not just your individual performance. Everybody must perform for Oracle to succeed." This recognition boosts a team orientation that the casual observer might not think compatible with Oracle's cutthroat reputation.

"The Oracle culture is highly competitive," Block said. "We all want to win. We all want to do a little bit better than the guy next to us. But this is also a very team-oriented culture, which I don't think you find in a lot of sales organizations. There's a pull for the greater cause and the greater good here."

We examine the link between having a greater cause and achieving long-term sales excellence in chapter 6, "Live the Mission." The priority Oracle places on a team orientation in fulfilling its own greater cause reflects the fact that the modern sales rep, especially in B2B, must know when and how to hand off to, or collaborate with, specialist sales colleagues and/or senior sales executives, and for those with global customers, colleagues located in different countries and steeped in different cultures around the world.

Speaking to the same point, Cisco's Rob Lloyd said that one of a modern sales organization's challenges is "developing leadership that can learn how to be collaborative, that can learn how to reach across the sales organization and share its collective talent." He continued, "It might not be you or your team's expert who needs to speak to the customer. It might be someone in a completely different group or different country." Moreover, the sales executives we spoke to agreed that it often falls to the field rep, as well as sales management, to recognize when such collaboration is necessary.

\* \* \*

To facilitate good teamwork, among other goals, several top-performing sales organizations recruit sales reps to serve on advisory councils and committees. Pitney Bowes rotates people from throughout its sales representative and sales management ranks for one-year assignments, in addition to their normal duties, on "a compensation advisory board and a marketing advisory team." This way, as a Pitney Bowes senior sales executive explained:

*It's not just some guy in the home office giving the sales force a comp plan or a marketing plan. We now have folks in the field who advo-*

*cate to their peers. So things are embraced a lot easier by the sales reps, as opposed to Moses coming down from the mountain and saying, 'I'm from the home office. Here's your marketing plan. Here's your compensation plan.'*

*Another thing it does is break down the civil war between different functions, especially between the field sales force and marketing. Everybody is forced to look at the world from each other's viewpoint. So the sales guy who thinks the zero-percent financing deal would be great on every product gets to understand why you really can't stay in business that way and have to use that on slow-moving products in inventory.*

Other sales organizations that have sales force representation on advisory and planning groups include Genzyme, Oracle, and Sony. At Sony, when a survey of sales reps' selling time showed they spent too much time on administrative tasks, the sales organization asked a committee of sales reps how to improve the situation. Recruiting sales reps to join in the sales organization's decision making is a form of finding and fostering leadership in the field that Sony's Ken Stevens called "keeping the field strong." As he put it:

*In sales, you keep your field strong because they're closest to the customer. They understand more of what's going on, and you have to empower them to make the calls and take the decisions.*

*When people say about the best sales talent, "Oh, those guys are great, they should move to headquarters," actually they shouldn't. They should stay in the field, closest to the customer. That's where they serve us best. You get the real deal of what's going on in a shorter period of time, the closer your best people are to the customer.*

At Genzyme, sales reps are empowered to help make decisions in an area usually thought of as management's exclusive domain: Hiring. Joe Brennan told us:

*We have a number of sales reps interview a prospective hire, so they have buy-in and mentorship responsibility from the beginning. We pass a little of the front-line management a step down, so the existing sales reps have a vested interest in helping the new sales reps*

15

*succeed. It's like they say it takes a village to raise a child. It's the same thing with sales.*

Relatedly, Brennan said, "We don't dictate how people do things in the field." And Sony's Ken Stevens told us, "Our sales organization is empowered to make decisions on the fly. We set a vision and overall objective, and we propose possible plans of action. But we allow the field to develop the steps of execution."

\* \* \*

Addressing the need to foster effective sales leadership and teamwork throughout an organization, Ron Boire, president and CEO of Brookstone and formerly a high-ranking executive at Toys "R" Us, Best Buy, and Sony Electronics, spoke of "servant leadership." No other interviewee mentioned the term "servant leadership," but the idea that leaders must serve the people they lead popped up again and again in our conversations. The head of sales at a global services firm said:

> *We work for the sales reps and the customers. Our more successful sales managers around the world have one critical ingredient other than intellect and drive and reflection of our values. It's that when they get up in the morning, they truly believe they work for the sales reps and customers.*

Similarly, sales leaders consistently said that their most important job is to coach. Oracle's rhetoric may generally stand out for its toughness, but recall Keith Block's comment, "If you're going to be a leader, you must learn how to teach. Your job is to teach."

\* \* \*

The comments of Keith Block and other senior sales executives made it very clear: Leadership excellence through collaboration applies not only within a sales organization but across the entire company. Block explained that he tells the Oracle sales reps:

> *If you need something to be successful, speak up. Don't just bury your head in the sand and say you couldn't make your number because of somebody else.*

*One thing I think our sales organization does very well is this: If it needs something from product development, it doesn't say, "Development didn't give it to me." It gets in Development's face and says, "We've got to make this happen for the customer."*

*And the great thing about the product development organization is that they're receptive. And so is marketing, and so is support. There is a mind-set that every line of business pulls for the customer. Every line of business knows that it can't succeed without somebody else working in a collaborative fashion.*

Again, we suggest that Oracle's "get[ting] in Development's face" rhetoric is far more adversarial than the collaborative behavior it calls for. As Block also told us, "I don't want sales managers. I want sales executives. I want people who don't think just about sales." Block insisted that while sales leaders must have "one eye on a sales number," they must also have "another eye on serving a market, making customers successful, and representing the company."

In discussing Oracle's model of having several sales specialists call on the same account, coordinated when necessary by a key account director, Keith Block observed that "no one person owns the customer relationship." And although the sales organization has "the front-line" responsibility for the customer relationship, the responsibility is not an exclusive one. Instead, the sales organization actively shares leadership on customer relationships with other functions within Oracle.

Again, we will see in chapter 3, "Advance the Science of Sales and the Art of the Customer Relationship, Part 1" that not all high-performing, customer-motivated sales organizations agree that the generalist sales person has become obsolete. No matter how they envision and define sales roles in terms of specialization, however, they agree that today's sales reps and managers must be able to lead from the front and hand off responsibility to colleagues as appropriate. By the same token, the modern sales organization has to make it easy for customers large and small to access appropriate firm resources, from sales to marketing to product development and supply chain.

The medium for addressing this issue at Oracle, Block said, is "a concept called a relationship plan. Basically, the best way to think of it is that it's a social contract between the customer and Oracle." MasterCard employs a similar model that it calls a "project charter." Oracle's relationship plan maps customer executives to Oracle executives in a cross-functional way, sets a schedule for reaching agreed-upon goals, and defines what both the customer and Oracle should expect of each other. "It's a living document that gets updated regularly and dictates how the two companies will work together." Although at first customers, "especially small customers that are new to Oracle and are a little intimidated or unclear about how to work with a big corporation," may look only to the sales organization for help, Block added:

> Over time the customers fan out and they build relationships with the support organization, they build relationships with the development organization, they build relationships with the marketing organization. So when they need something, they don't need to go through the account team. They can go right to the executive in marketing that they've been working with, or the executive in development or the executive in support.
>
> It works incredibly well. It also helps when there are multiple sales reps in the account. It's a wonderful way to set the rules of engagement for everyone.

Similarly, Block's own senior sales management team is also cross-functional and includes "people who are not actually in my organization." Representatives from Oracle's finance and human resources (HR) organizations participate in "collaborative" decision making for the sales organization, debating strategies and tactics in "a very open style."

* * *

In today's B2B sales, leading by collaboration, rather than by command and control, increasingly includes collaboration with customers. In contrast to its 1990s practice of pushing products out "without a lot of customer input and feedback," Oracle now works to "institutionalize customer loyalty," Keith Block told us, by heeding customers' desires for "control, a vote, and a voice" in how Oracle's products and services function. The result is that the company has moved to what "really is customer-driven development for our software."

One way collaboration occurs is through direct interactions between the sales organization and leading companies in their industries, such as Alcoa,

Ingersoll Rand, and Pella Windows. Block said, "We've invested very heavily in these companies, and they've reciprocated. They've invested very heavily in us, not just from a revenue perspective, but in helping us to develop products based on their industry expertise."

The give and take between Oracle and customer companies may go beyond specific products to larger issues. Pella, for example, "is pushing us to put clean manufacturing principles into our software." Because of the benefits Pella derives from its close relationship with Oracle, it hosts an annual event at its headquarters in Pella, IA, for "about 200 Oracle customers," where "they talk about our software, how to work with Oracle, and what the relationship is all about."

For Oracle there are twin payoffs from relationships with industry-leading customers. First, there is "a lot of mutual learning, which is the true measure of a win–win relationship." This helps keep Oracle product capabilities and benefits on the leading edge of information technology (IT). Equally important, it extends customer trust. After the sales organization has won the deal "by proving the value of Oracle products in return on investment and total cost of ownership," customers know that "we're going to make sure that they continue to get value, because they're going to help us innovate, they're going to be able to influence how we develop the product."

The second payoff is the ability to do "reference selling." Block explained:

> *If you get the top tier, you can go to the broader market and say, "You know what? The top 10 companies in your industry all run their businesses on Oracle." That reference selling is enormous.*

When Oracle has identified a new customer segment or product category as a growth area — like security solutions — it concentrates its initial efforts on sales to leading companies. "Winning the first reference is huge," Block said. "Because now you can say, 'We did security for such and such a company. Why don't you talk to them?' It's very, very powerful stuff."

As an example of leveraging interactions with important customers and potential customers, Block said that he had just returned from meeting the vice provost and chief information officer of "a world-class university with a fantastic computer science department and a home-grown student information system." Ultimately, the meeting was "a conversation about risk:"

Would the university be better off "buying something off somebody's shelf" or relying on its own resources and open-source software to manage student information?

Block proposed a third possibility, that Oracle "disclose what our future plans are for student information systems" and that the university "tell us what's important" from its point of view. He continued:

> *That's the sort of conversation the customer wants to have. Can they influence where Oracle is taking its software? If the answer is yes, and there's a good feeling about managing the risk and they're going to get return on investment in value, that's actually a pretty easy sell.*

We mentioned previously Keith Block's visits to a customer "in a very remote location." Here, too, Block said, a key element in winning the sale was that the customer could in effect co-develop the products that Oracle would be installing over a long period of time. The company "is a leader in their industry, they have incredible intellectual property, and they want to put some of that intellectual property into our products." Oracle could not have made the deal without world-class product development, to be sure, but it also could not have succeeded without the sales organization's ability to deploy its intellectual capital to engage customers as partners. "They view buying our applications as a lifetime decision," Block explained, "and they had to be sure we have the right cultural fit as well as the horses to do what they're looking for."

Beyond one-to-one interactions with industry-leading companies, Oracle has recruited a broad range of customers to participate in "over 400 advisory boards." The advisory boards cover functional product areas and specific industry needs. They give participants "a voice and a vote" on "what's really important to their company and their industry … [and] what they want to see baked into the software." Likewise, the advisory boards give Oracle opportunities to learn what is currently important to customers, pick up on new industry trends in their early stages, and extend reference selling through multiple customer segments.

\*\*\*

Plainly, the ethos of "leading from the front" does not involve any reluctance to delegate and share leadership authority not only throughout the sales organization but even with customers. To be effective, sharing leadership throughout an organization requires good recruiting, selecting, and training, a subject we consider in chapter 2, "Speak Clearly — and Carry a Big Carrot." As that title phrase indicates, it also demands good communication.

# Silence is Bad

In the average sales organization, leadership's communication exemplifies the worst pitfalls of the command-and-control approach. The communication is all one-way and there is too little of it: A kick-off sales meeting followed by a string of memos from headquarters. The pattern is very different at high-performing sales organizations. Oracle, for example, follows a cadence of frequent formal and informal sales communications that in their totality are very much a two-way street.

"Every year at the kick-off meeting, we establish a rallying cry," Keith Block said. But as already noted, each year's rallying cry serves the "longer-term plan" of "relationship, solutions, service." Thereafter, Block heads at least one quarterly "all-hands call" for the entire sales organization (marketing is invited but not required to participate). This may be more frequent organization-wide communication than occurs in most companies, but "it sets the tone, it sets the pace" for interim results and "what we're going to achieve in the next 90 days."

Each call lasts an hour or so, providing time for "lots of recognition" of good work by the sales organization as a whole, by account teams, and by individual sales reps. The call also provides time for "scolding," however, on the rare occasions when the organization underperforms.

Asked if he sweetens bad news with good news, Block said, "I'm a big believer in that very simple principle. But more importantly, if there's good news to tell, you tell good news; if there are areas to focus on, you tell them." The rule here, Block said, is that once problems are resolved, they should be forgotten and never held over anyone's head:

> Thankfully, the very few times I have had to say, "Look, you know what, we stumbled," the team has responded.
>
> A perfect example was a while back, for the first time in five years, we didn't have double-digit growth in the quarter. It was Q2 and we just missed it. We didn't execute. It is what it is.

*So I had the call after the quarter was over, and I said, "You know what? We didn't execute. Here are the things we need to focus on."*

*I was angry, and everybody who was on that call knew that I was angry. I said, "This is not the organization that's been putting it up for 10 years. We got sloppy. We can't do that. We're the engine for the whole company, we have a responsibility to customers, we are part of something really big here."*

*We announced our Q3 results, and the first thing I said on the next all-hands call was, "Nobody will ever talk about Q2 again. It's dead. Nobody cares. You guys just nailed it. We had a fantastic Q3. We're back to our rightful place." They respond to that.*

The anecdote exemplifies much of what we discussed with Keith Block: Willingness to grapple with tough issues, personal accountability to a team and its shared goals, passionate commitment to make things right, the readiness to teach others how to do so, and a sense of the larger mission served by the sales organization.

The great benefits of quarterly all-hands calls are their consistency and directness. But they are primarily one-way communications and must be supplemented, Block said, echoing his counterparts at other high-performing sales organizations, by two-way communications and "lots of listening." In leading from the front, Block and his senior sales management team continually strive to engage the sales force, one-on-one and in small groups, in "safe harbor, open dialogue that's not going to get back" in an identifiable way to the sales reps' immediate bosses. Block elaborated:

*If I'm traveling to meet with customers in Dallas, say, and there's a dinner open, I'll do a round table for everybody who's not with a customer or doesn't have a family commitment at home.*

*We go out to dinner and just rap sales. At first people often don't want to talk, and I have an expression, "Silence is bad. If you don't speak up, I can't fix it." You loosen them up, and you really learn a lot.*

*These guys are out there on the front line every single day. If their lives are miserable, they're not going to be productive. You've got to listen to them.*

Although Block did not make it a special point, we cannot fail to observe allowing for the possibility that sales reps' family commitments may occasionally prevent them from attending these round tables. Oracle is clearly a hard-nosed place, but it also has a softer side with respect to what one senior sales executive described as "the care and feeding of your people."

The Oracle sales organization's concern for its people is genuine, but not altruistic. It serves the business. Block said:

> *Numbers are great. I have all the reports and portals and metrics to stare at that you can imagine. Pipeline, quarter-over-quarter growth, year-over-year growth, product groupings — it's all the natural stuff. I can tell you what my business is at any minute.*

> *But candidly, the thing I go on most is talking to the customers and talking to the field. We've got all the great technology in the world to report the numbers. But for me really to have my hand on the pulse of the business, I have to be out there, talking to the customers and talking to the field sales reps.*

We heard similar comments from executives at other elite sales organizations. Earlier we mentioned sales leaders' consensus that their organizations will fail if they don't hear things directly from sales reps and customers. One of the main reasons Genzyme established a sales and marketing advisory committee that includes sales reps was to become "better at listening" to the sales force. "You don't always have to please sales reps," Genzyme's Joe Brennan said, "but you have to listen to them" to keep a sales organization functioning at a high level. Likewise, Cisco's Rob Lloyd told us that "a culture of listening helps positive change to occur." This requires "open communication, where nobody gets punished" for raising difficult issues.

At Sony, Ken Stevens told us, there is "a very formal process" of senior sales leaders' visits to field sales offices for meetings with sales reps. Equally important on these visits is "management by wandering around." Stevens continued:

> *When I visit sales offices I spend a lot of time wandering around and sitting and talking with people. It might not be about the business. It might be about whatever happened in the news or somebody's favorite sports team, putting them in a position where they recognize we are all the same and we all do the same job.*

*Information piles out of those informal conversations because people are comfortable. They say, "You know what, I can't figure such and such out." And I offer suggestions about what to try or who to talk to. Or I say, "Let me take that back and we'll find an answer."*

To enhance the sales organization's listening to the field and to encourage collaborative, "peer-to-peer" communication between sales reps, Stevens established an internal blog. He elaborated:

*All senior management must log on to the blog and read it. So people recognize a couple of things. Number one, they can communicate in the way they prefer to communicate, not necessarily my preferred method. It's not a memo from my office. Number two, they know I read it and management reads it, and they get answers on it from management as well as from the other sales reps. So you don't just say you listen, you demonstrate that you listen.*

Twice a year Stevens meets the sales organization's "field training group, a bunch of kids out of college," who work with retailers on displays and help train their staffs on interacting with consumers. The average meeting is "10 minutes of presentation and 90 minutes of Q&A," Stevens said. "That group is fearless. They deal with retailers and consumers every day, and they ask the questions that everybody wants answered." Stevens underscored that the meetings are at least as much about what he learns as what the field training group learns: "I do that twice a year to make sure I know what's going on."

For Sony, this activity follows one of the central precepts of its co-founder and most famous CEO, Akio Morita: "Wisdom is not the sole possession of management." Stevens said, "Wisdom doesn't get housed exclusively here at headquarters. I talk about keeping the field strong, because we don't have all the answers here."

As the chorus of sales executives' commentary linking leadership and listening makes clear, the view that "wisdom is not the sole possession of management" is not the sole possession of Sony, either. It is shared by all highly successful sales organizations and is embodied in their daily leadership practices.

# *Conclusion*

Summing up his view of sales leadership, Oracle's Keith Block told us:

> *Historically, there are different styles of leadership. But the one that appeals the most to me, and that I think is most applicable to our sales organization, is not leading from behind, it's leading from the front. It's getting out there with the troops and saying, "I'm not going to ask you to do anything I'm not going to do. If you're going to do this, I'm going to do it with you." I think that's really important.*

There is no question that everything Oracle does it does with its characteristic "in your face" style. Yet beneath the rhetorical differences are underlying similarities between Oracle and other consistently excellent sales organizations. Leading from the front typifies the otherwise varied management styles we observed in sales organizations that, year in and year out, rank at or near the top of their industries and markets.

At the beginning of the chapter, we said that the most important aspect of leading from the front is the ability and willingness of sales leaders, and a sales organization as a whole, to venture into areas of complexity and risk in order to create new ways of identifying and meeting customer needs. The sales organizations we highlight offer many pertinent examples.

Consider Oracle's development of new IT security solutions or Keith Block's "conversation about risk" with a customer, both mentioned earlier, or J&J's development of new, often lifesaving, medical products and surgical techniques (see chapter 6, "Live the Mission"); or Cisco's identification of adjacent product areas as it migrates out from its core networking products (see chapter 5, "Make Loud Mistakes").

Sony Electronics and Whirlpool offer two of the most illuminating examples of venturing into areas of complexity and risk, from the perspective of a sales organization as well as its customers. Each sales organization was the first in its industry to recognize and exploit a transformative new sales model, bravely abandoning a familiar sell-in approach for lean inventory, logistics-based sell-through. The result was dramatically greater profitability for the two sales organizations and their respective customers (see chapter 4, "Advance the Science of Sales and the Art of the Customer Relationship, Part 2").

The lesson is clear. Lead from the front. Lead by example and in collaboration with your sales management team, your sales reps, your cross-functional colleagues, and your customers, and you will be well on the way to outpacing your competition.

## HOW GREAT SALES ORGANIZATIONS SEED SUCCESS BY LEADING FROM THE FRONT

- Spend lots of time in the field to observe, inspect, teach, coach, and sell.
- Lead by example and in collaboration with the sales force and cross-functional colleagues.
- Develop leadership throughout the organization and ensure effective hand-offs between leaders at all levels, from front-line sales managers to senior executives.
- Build great teamwork.
- Foster "acting like it's your own business," empowering salespeople to take initiative in crafting and delivering customer value.
- Lead by listening, developing business and market insight that gives meaning to the numbers by engaging both the sales organization and customers in two-way communication.
- Are the first to enter areas of market risk and complexity to innovate new ways of delivering customer value and spearhead sales model and organizational change.

# CHAPTER 2
# Speak Clearly — and Carry a Big Carrot

**JOB ONE FOR SALES LEADERS**, from front-line sales managers to senior sales executives, is fostering great individual and team performance throughout the organization. The right game plan is worthless if the players can't execute.

How do the best sales organizations meet this all-important challenge? We found that the top sales organizations:

- Make hiring and training a consistent priority.

- Treat HR expenditures as an investment in the sales organization's, and the entire firm's, future.

- View selling as a training ground for general management as well as sales management.

- Manage the sales force by activity, not only by results.

- Devote substantial effort and ingenuity to reward and recognition programs that align financial incentives with satisfying customers' needs and inspire a commitment to sales excellence.

- Deal with the sales force in a spirit of tough love, supporting and empowering salespeople in combination with clear expectations, limits, and scorecards.

\* \* \*

Theodore Roosevelt famously said, "Speak softly and carry a big stick." It's a memorable twist on the carrot and stick method, which has had many adherents down through the ages. In other words, be nice as long as that works, and respond to uncooperative or undesired behavior with force and punishment. But is this the best way to get a sales organization to work individually and collectively for a larger mission and rally to managers who lead from the front? Is it a good recipe for handling HR issues such as hiring, training, and performance management?

The problem with carrot and stick methods, behavioral science and organizational psychology have shown, and experienced managers all know from daily experience, is that this approach only works in the short term. In the long term, punishment eclipses reward and breeds resentment and distrust. As a practical matter, a senior sales executive we spoke to for this book observed, it is hard to keep carrot and stick from degenerating into "all stick and no carrot." Referring to the dysfunctional state of his current sales organization when he first took it over, he said:

> *The big stick approach can't be sustained, because it only works when you have the stick and you step on their throat and say, "Okay, that quarter is done, now what are you going to do for me this quarter?" As long as you step harder each quarter you can sustain most of that, but as soon as you take your foot off their throat, it's gone.*
>
> *Not just displaced, it's gone. It speaks in values you can't predict. When you take your eye off the ball, they're not going to be working in the business's best interest, because they don't really feel a part of it.*

Poor communication — hectoring, inconsistent, infrequent, and one-way — is a hallmark of dysfunctional organizations that use a heavy stick on their people. They are not places with a clear larger mission or where senior management leads from the front.

By contrast, the most successful sales organizations speak clearly and frequently to their people, both collectively and one-on-one, and listen to them carefully. These organizations also favor the carrot over the stick. Stating a view that was echoed over and over again in our interviews, Greg Lorden of SAP Business Objects told us that the best way to extract consistent high performance is "with an investment in your people."

A senior sales executive in the healthcare industry described these activities as "the care and feeding of your people." Describing Oracle's successful transition to solution selling, Keith Block told us, "We treat our people better now. And I think you have to do that." FedEx prides itself on having been a "people first" company since its founding.

This does not mean any lack of toughness in performance management. Rather, we believe that the sales organizations profiled in this book practice "tough love" in developing and deploying their people. Sony's Ken Stevens said, "Sometimes you have to, in a respectful way, deliver a well-intentioned kick in the butt. That's okay, because I had my share." Finally, the stick is always there to be used in the form of denied reward and recognition or letting people go when they consistently underperform. As Oracle's Keith Block put it, "If somebody is consistently performing poorly quarter after quarter, well, you're either going to be the right guy in the job or you're not going to be the right guy."

In their HR practices, great sales organizations accordingly concentrate on:

- Smart hiring
- Good initial and ongoing training for both sales reps and front-line sales managers
- Management by activity rather than short-term results
- Effective reward and recognition programs

When these elements all align with both sales goals and the organization's larger mission, they add up to, in the words of Tom Schmitt, FedEx Solutions senior vice president, "getting the right people doing the right things in the right way." (Before going further, we should note that we discuss hiring and training in relation to a sales organization's larger mission in chapter 6, "Live the Mission," and that discussion is also relevant here. Likewise, chapter 1, "Lead from the Front," also bears on these issues with regard to pushing leadership down through the sales organization and the need for sales leaders to be teachers and mentors.)

## *Smart Hiring: Attitude, Intellect, and Integrity*

When we spoke about sales excellence with sales leaders across industries, a common theme was that, as one executive at a major telecommunications company put it, "Hiring is the most important thing you do. Period. End of story."

For some sales leaders this means looking for new hires who have what one of them called "sales DNA." For others it means looking for problem solvers and then teaching them good selling techniques.

Executives at high-performing sales organizations all agreed, however, that salespeople must be entrepreneurial, creative, and resilient. In a world of over-supply and under-demand in virtually every sector of the economy, the road to a sale is usually paved with tough rejections. So salespeople must be able, Sony's Ken Stevens said, to "adapt and overcome" in the mutual interest of the customer, the sales organization, and themselves.

In chapter 1, "Lead from the Front," we discussed how executives at high-performing sales organizations foster creative initiative and entrepreneurship throughout their organizations. Recall, for example, that Oracle's Keith Block wants everyone in the sales organization to "act like it's [their] own business," with even the most "coin-operated sales reps" doing so in a customer-motivated way.

SAP Business Objects' Greg Lorden told us he looks for "a blue-collar mind set" in new hires, whether they are just starting out or already accomplished salespeople. He elaborated:

> The rep with the blue-collar mind set says, "I'm going to get some doors slammed on me on this. It's up to me to think of something creative. The lead script they gave me is not working, so I've got to change it."

> I have that blue-collar mind set conversation with 90 percent of the people I interview. One guy was leaving a competitor to come here. He had a stellar reputation, but I told him, "Our team is world-class. If you're done growing and learning, this is not a good place for you. What are you going to do to make an impact here and set a new standard?"

> Three months later he said, "I cannot stop thinking about where I can make an impact." He's been here two years, and he's been phenomenal. He was going to be phenomenal anyway, but we probably got another 10 or 15 percent out of him. People saw him doing that and they said, "Why is he here working late? He's already arrived. I better turn up my game."

\* \* \*

Despite the increasing complexity of sales roles, especially in B2B, and despite the heavy responsibility for an entire company's health that sales bears, especially in tough economic times, some still consider sales a last resort career for those who don't have enough talent and smarts to do anything else. Or as David Smith, vice president of global sales and marketing at J&J's eyecare subsidiary, Vistakon, put it, "Sales has typically been considered kind of the red-haired stepchild in terms of business sophistication."

Anyone who looks closely at today's sales challenges can quickly see what is terribly wrong with this opinion. Only by deploying substantial intellectual capital can sales organizations collectively and salespeople individually create value for the customer and value for their own firms. This book is rich in examples of top sales organizations' intellectual capital. In the present context, Dave Edmonds, FedEx senior vice president for worldwide services, observed that the hiring of sales reps must be "highly selective" in large part because of the intellectual demands of the job. To show that FedEx's logistics capabilities justify premium pricing, and can actually save customers significant amounts of money and speed their growth by furnishing greater control of supply chain issues, "your value quantification has got to be sharp, because you're not going to go into a CFO and lay out a comparison to an income statement and balance sheet and expect to win the deal unless you're absolutely right and you have bullet-proof numbers."

In addition to meeting the increasingly complex demands of the sales job, high-performing sales organizations look for intellectual ability in job candidates so as to find individuals who can rise to take on leadership roles within the sales organization and the company itself. As we'll see in chapter 6, "Live the Mission," Vistakon and other J&J subsidiaries concentrate their recruiting on college campuses precisely because, as Vistakon's David Smith said, "We are not just hiring sales reps. We are hiring our future sales managers and business leaders... . [Sales] is just as sophisticated as any other functionality, and you can develop some great general business managers out of the sales function."

Executives at other high-performing sales organizations voiced similar views, and later we look closely at how Whirlpool raised the level of its new hires.

Ultimately, perhaps, good salespeople are boundary spanners. They live and think within the customer's world, while at the same time also living and thinking from within the sales organization's point of view. Like fluent bilingual speakers, they can instantaneously translate between these two perspectives.

* * *

Great sales organizations look for people of integrity who share their values and will embrace a larger, customer-motivated mission. By the same token, the most talented job candidates want to work for companies whose larger mission includes doing good in the world.

Kim Metcalf-Kupres, vice president for global sales and marketing at Johnson Controls, noted how one of the key bonds between her company and the sales force is a shared commitment to environmental sustainability. Cisco's Rob Lloyd pointed out that employees and prospective hires have an "increasing interest in corporate social responsibility." And Brookstone CEO Ron Boire emphasized that good long-term performance rests on employees being able to "identify with the company and know that its values are in line with theirs."

FedEx's Tom Schmitt said that the company looks for new hires who "have the DNA to go above and beyond for the customer." Sony Electronics similarly prizes sales reps who express their entrepreneurial spirit, Ken Stevens said, with "creative ideas" that "make the case for doing good business" by "do[ing] what's right for the customer — and then some."

How does a sales organization find and attract such people? Even in an economic downturn, competition continues for the best talent. In chapter 6, "Live the Mission," we shall see how J&J's Vistakon subsidiary concentrates its recruiting efforts at better colleges and universities, framing entry-level sales not only as stimulating and rewarding work on its own terms but as a gateway to higher-level jobs in sales and other functions. Other top sales organizations, such as Whirlpool, whose distinctive recruiting and training practices we examine later in this chapter, position themselves in much the same way.

Stepping back to take a macro view, we believe that a sales organization's commitment to customer-motivated excellence is its most powerful recruiting tool. As we explore in chapter 6, "Live the Mission," sales leaders consistently spoke of a larger mission's importance for both existing and prospective employees. Organizations that also exude a spirit of shared leadership, strive to deal with and nurture salespeople as individuals, combine scientific rigor with a human touch, and understand that mistakes are a necessary part of developing best practices will stand out as good places to work. Such organizations become talent magnets and always have an edge on the competition in hiring the cream of the crop.

## *Training the Sales Force*

As the complexity of the sales role has increased, so has the need for effective training. But because training is expensive and its results, for good or ill, frequently do not show up immediately, it often draws a cost-cutting eye, especially in rough economic times. Ron Boire warned, "It's so easy to cut training, because the results don't come for a long, long time. But you've got to believe in — what's that equation I forgot from business school — total factor productivity. It's capital, technology, and training."

Consistent winners among sales organizations resist the temptation to reduce training. These are true learning organizations, focusing on both initial training for novice salespeople and ongoing training to keep the sales force as a whole up-to-date and able to adapt to changing market conditions or new sales models.

No sales organization can ignore cost considerations, however, and savvy sales leaders make every effort to get the most out of limited training budgets, including using distance e-learning. But the sales leaders we spoke to agreed that it is important to bring salespeople together in training sessions to build esprit de corps and, as one executive said, "create and sustain a culture .... If you teach the skills, but you don't instill that belief and loyalty, you've just created some really great talent for someone else." For example, Xerox, long renowned for its sales training, has over 5,000 online courses available to the sales force but continues to bring salespeople together for face-to-face training.

Smart hiring helps make training more effective. Elaborating on the importance of a "blue-collar mind-set," SAP Business Objects' Greg Lorden recalled how "two of our best sales reps recently came up to me at kick-off, at different times on the same evening, and said, 'I want to turn up my game this year, I want to get better.' If you're a sales leader, you cannot hear anything better."

Following initial training, many sales organizations assign novice sales reps to inside support or telesales roles. Keith Block told us Oracle views inside sales as "a good place to groom people to go into the field. They prove their mettle there. They learn about the Oracle culture, they learn about our solutions for customers. You can see how they perform and say, 'Yes, that one's got a future in the field. Let's see what we can do there.'"

Adapting to new sales models presents a special training challenge. When Hewlett-Packard (HP) decided to shift its sales force to specialist solution selling, it instituted a rigorous "license to practice" program run by Sales Operations. The program involves sales reps participating in simulation exercises in front of their peers. HP's Andy Mattes described how "at the beginning of the training, senior salespeople are so nervous" about their colleagues' reactions that "their voices crack. And these are people who have no fear in front of the customer." The intensity of the training produces "an intense level of effort and commitment."

Similarly, when Honeywell Building Solutions (HBS) embarked on a turnaround effort, Kevin Madden, vice president for global sales, and his leadership team compiled "detailed playbooks" for the sales reps. As Madden explained:

> *The failure mode before our turnaround effort began was that no one had a plan. So we really put a lot of rigor into coaching sessions around the playbooks. How many first calls you need to make, how many requirements sessions you need to set up, how many letters of intent you have to draft, how many jobs you need to be negotiating, how many quotes you need to make per week, how many prospects you need to have in your funnel and pipeline at all points — really keying in on the activity management that leads to success.*

One innovative feature of the training program has become an integral part of HBS's sales process. Madden continued:

> *Something I think is ingenious and really brought our sales teams together is what we call impact reviews on jobs over $750,000. We bring a team together of peers within the sales organization and ask, "All right, can you really speak the customer's language?" It strengthens the organization in articulating customer drivers, not generic capabilities. We want to focus on understanding and meeting real needs, not pitching a product or service.*

> *And then the impact review also asks, "Can you articulate the customer's next best alternative?" So we also strengthen our ability to differentiate ourselves from the competition in the space we're serving.*

The impact reviews include learning by doing in actual customer engagements — "going live" in HBS parlance. Madden said:

> *If we feel the quarterback on the sales team starts exaggerating, we say, "Let's go live. Get the customer on the phone, and tell them what we're doing." And then I or another sales leader will get on the call and say, "We're looking at your account now, and we want to make sure we understand your drivers. Here's what we believe*

*our capabilities are to hit the needs you have and the drivers in your industry, and here's why we think it's the best solution. We're trying to figure out what our next steps are, and the lead rep on your account said such and such. Is this right?"*

*The playbooks and impact reviews have given us a huge lift. They've become a core competency at HBS.*

As evidence, Madden pointed out that sales reps themselves now initiate informal impact reviews with local and regional sales managers for jobs smaller than $750,000. The sales reps do it "because they're winning so much business as a result."

Some sales situations require very specific competencies. In chapter 6, "Live the Mission," we examine how J&J provides training in medical specialties and subspecialties for sales reps selling in those areas. In chapter 4, "Advance the Science of Sales and the Art of the Customer Relationship, Part 2" we examine how Sony Electronics transformed its sales model from sell-in to sell-through and in the process transformed its relationship with retailers by training its sales force in supply-chain logistics.

Another challenge is that effective training for the entire sales force may not be sufficient to maximize the output of the best salespeople, whose efforts represent a disproportionate share of sales revenue and profit. Several sales executives emphasized to us that, in the words of Oracle's Keith Block, "even great athletes need guidance to focus on the right things."

For this reason MasterCard regularly singles out high-potential salespeople for participation in "cross-integrated work streams" with colleagues from other functions. This has two benefits, MasterCard's Gary Flood explained. It instills "a financial, commercial, business development acumen" that bolsters key account management. Exposing top salespeople to colleagues in other functions also "builds relationships between the sales organization and our internal partners."

# *Whirlpool Real Whirled*

One of the most intriguing and illuminating examples of sales rep training we encountered was at Whirlpool. When Sam Abdelnour, vice president for North American sales, took over the sales organization, where he had spent most of his career, he knew that he needed to change its makeup. The problem was not low performance. Indeed, the organization was highly capable and put up great numbers year in and year out. But it was aging and did not reflect the increasing diversity in consumer demographics. Abdelnour believed that over the long term this demographic disconnect would hamper Whirlpool's ability to help its trade customers communicate with consumers effectively.

Abdelnour explained:

> When I first took over the selling organization, I sat down with my HR director, and we looked at an organization that was performing at a very high level. But I said, "You know, I've been at Whirlpool 22 years, and just about every one of these guys has been here longer than I have."

> I got HR's report back, and it demonstrated that I had an extremely aged selling organization. About 70 percent of my salespeople and about 75 percent of my sales managers were over fifty years old. And about 88 percent were white males.

> I told my people, "Guys, you're the most successful selling organization in our industry right now. You prove it every day. But my fear is not that you're getting too old to execute, but that you're going to want to retire before I'm ready for you to retire. We have to start developing a new pool of people."

The answer Abdelnour and his colleagues devised was "Whirlpool Real Whirled," inspired by MTV's "Real World," the reality television show in which a group of young people out on their own for the first time are filmed living together in a group house. For Whirlpool's version of "Real World," Sam Abdelnour told us:

> We hire fresh college graduates only, no graduate students. Each Real Whirled class has an average of eight people and has to be a minimum of 50 percent diverse. They live in a house together for eight weeks. They do their own cooking, their own cleaning, and they get their training there.

> They have to entertain Whirlpool people every night and cook them a meal. That's how they get to know people from different parts of the company.

> We change the appliances every week so that not only do they use all of our appliances but they also use our competitors' appliances

*as well. At the end of the eight weeks, they know not only what products are available from the appliance industry but also how they all work.*

*Hopefully, their preferences are Whirlpool brands. But if they're not, we get good feedback for engineering and design about what works and what doesn't."*

For the first Whirlpool Real Whirled classes, the company had "a difficult time" attracting high-quality applicants. The technology bubble was still expanding, and "everyone coming out of college wanted to go to work in Silicon Valley and become an instant Internet millionaire. So in the beginning it was friends of family, kids of Whirlpool employees." When that bubble exploded, everything changed. "For the average class of eight places, today we get two hundred applicants."

Whirlpool now runs six to 10 Real Whirled classes a year, "because we've got such a huge need for more people as our sales model progresses." The Whirlpool Real Whirled graduates become "market brand reps" (MBRs) and go to work supporting direct sellers while continuing to receive further training. "If they're successful after fourteen months, then they move on to a sales responsibility where they actually have a quota and earn a commission."

Speaking about the youth of these hires, Sam Abdelnour continued:

*In most cases, they literally move from their dorm rooms into the Whirlpool Real Whirled house. That's how young they are.*

*The reason we don't hire MBAs in this program is that they're not as receptive to this kind of immersive learning. They've got higher expectations as to who they are and what they should be. And I can't build a sales organization based on the expectations of 28-year-old MBAs coming out of business school.*

*The golden apple for the Real Whirled kids is that five years, six years on, if they're successful, we'll send them to business school and we'll pay for it.*

The results of Whirlpool Real Whirled have been so good that "we have about 98.5 percent retention back to class one." As for the program's diversity goals, Sam Abdelnour said, "My selling organization now is 67 percent diverse, versus where we were before at 12 percent. So it's been a great success story not only in that regard but in giving us confidence that we're building a future for the selling organization." And although the program was designed to create talent for sales, it has become "a feeder pool for the entire company."

This story reflects the excellence of the company's sales training and the increasingly rigorous and strategic aspects of B2B sales functions, as well as, echoing the words of colleague David Provost, Director of Sales Development, the weight that sales has traditionally carried within Whirlpool. As Sam Abdelnour put it, "I don't care if you want to be in finance or supply chain or marketing or procurement or product development. You will be better in any of those areas of the business, if you have carried the sales bag for a while and learned to understand the trade, the consumer, and how appliances are sold one at a time."

## *Training the Sales Manager*

Consider these statements:

- "The sales manager, that first level above the people in the trenches everyday, plays the most pivotal role in any sales organization."

- "The most important people in our sales organization are the front-line sales managers."

- "The front-line manager's coaching is the biggest key to success."

- "The key (to our success) is the front-line sales manager."

- "The front-line sales manager … has the most important role in the sales organization…. That job is critical."

- "The most important relationship in the sales organization is the relationship between the front-line sales manager and the rep."

We could easily go on and on. Every sales executive we interviewed made a similar statement about the pivotal importance of the front-line sales manager. Dan Regan, Genzyme Renal's head of sales, spoke to this issue in part by recalling a sales manager's influence on him early in his career:

> *When I was a young field rep at J&J, I had a manager by the name of Jeff Bailey. Jeff was phenomenal. Like everybody else I knew at the company, I would get nervous and think, "Oh, God, Jeff's coming to work with me for two days. Got to have the car cleaned and all that." After Jeff left at the end of the two days, I was sky-high, because*

*he had made me better. We had gotten some things accomplished, and also he had given me a couple of things to work on.*

*The next time he came out with me, I wanted to show him, "Hey, I've been working on those things. Here they are. Let's make sure I'm getting better there." A good manager leaves people feeling good and motivated.*

Accordingly, elite sales organizations take great pains in choosing and developing front-line sales managers. The high-performing sales rep is not necessarily a good candidate. "To assume that is a death spiral," one sales executive said of an organization that had done so. Although above-average sales ability is necessary to do the job well, Dan Regan said it is equally important "that the front-line sales manager has the ability to coach. It's somebody that feels empowered to coach as well, somebody that is comfortable having the pat-people-on-the-back conversation as well as the tough conversation."

In chapter 1, "Lead from the Front," we saw that senior executives at top-performing sales organizations see coaching and teaching as the number-one job at all levels of sales management. But the level at which that is most important on a daily basis, they also agree, is that of the front-line sales manager. For example, Fedex's Tom Schmitt described the front-line manager's job as helping the team succeed "first and foremost by coaching and secondly by helping teammates through the tough jobs."

Successful sales organizations thus strive to preserve and enhance the coaching time of their front-line managers. Many seek measurable base-lines and track improvement through sales–time surveys, which may become the basis for reassigning administrative and sales support duties from both sales managers and sales reps to dedicated sales support or sales operations groups. We touch on this issue later and discuss it more fully in chapter 3, "Advance the Science of Selling and the Art of the Customer Relationship, Part 1."

Here we want to mention a few examples of what Dan Regan called "managing the manager." In Genzyme's own case, this means that:

*The second-line manager asks the front-line manager, "What does your work session look like? Let me see your post-work session field-conference report. Let's talk about what you talked about with the rep, let's look at the reviews you are doing."*

*If everything is wonderful, and there is nothing for this person to work on, I do not need a second-line manager. There should be something that we can be helping the front-line manager with. Even if it is, "Hey, you are doing this really well, here are three different ways to do more of it," that is important. It is just letting them know that good coaching is the expectation, and helping them understand that people benefit from that and want it. At the end of the day, the sales reps really want feedback. They want coaching.*

Just as it has "license to practice" training programs for salespeople, HP also has "license to manage" programs for sales managers, with simulation exercises in which the managers participate in front of their peers. HP's Andy Mattes told us, "We noticed we had to train sales managers even more than salespeople."

Likewise, just as HBS has "detailed playbooks" for sales reps, it also has them for sales leaders. One of the barriers to the successful turnaround that HBS achieved was that each sales manager was responsible for too many sales reps. According to Kevin Madden, the result was that "our front-line sales leaders became nothing more than administrators. So no coaching and no learning were going on, just responding." It was essential to reduce the span of control from 18–25 sales reps per front-line sales leader to 8–12 sales reps per leader. Only when that was done could HBS achieve its goal of having front-line sales leaders "spend at least half their time coaching sales reps and participating in customer engagements."

\* \* \*

Front-line sales managers who excel at empowering salespeople and coaching them to better performance naturally form a pool of candidates for upper-level sales management. Mike MacDonald, Xerox corporate senior vice president, told us, "If you look at all of our senior vice presidents in sales, the one thing they all have in common is that they were all very good front-line managers."

In chapter 6, "Live the Mission," we look at J&J's "leadership roadmap" for manager development. For its part, Xerox often sends rising sales executives to the renowned Center for Creative Leadership in North Carolina. At SAP Business Objects, Greg Lorden makes a concerted effort to teach leadership and show his management team "how to do my job."

In chapter 1, "Lead from the Front," we mentioned Cisco's concern for "developing leadership that can learn how to be collaborative, that can learn how to reach across the sales organization and share its collective talent." Its sales organization does this, Cisco's Rob Lloyd shared with us, by tapping promising local and regional sales managers for "cross-functional" teams that address such challenges as entering new markets.

With regard to senior sales leadership as well as front-line sales managers, top-performing organizations above all stress the desire and willingness to coach and empower employees. Speaking to this point, Ron Boire shared the experience of interviewing two people for a vice president's position and asking them both, "Do you believe that everyone wants to do a good job?" Boire continued, "One of them said yes and one of them said no. So one was an attitude of growth, and one was an attitude of supervision and punishment. I want the first, I don't want the second."

To explain why, Boire hearkened back to an incident he observed as a sales leader at Best Buy, when he accompanied his colleague and future Best Buy CEO Brian Dunn on a surprise store visit:

> *This guy comes running from the back of the store — and Best Buy stores are big, they're 45,000 square feet — and said, "Brian, it's so good to see you. You haven't been here in such a long time. We've been making the store look great."*

> *And it became apparent that this was a special needs person. Over 10 years earlier he had worked directly for Brian, and Brian had invested in him. That investment, I guarantee, has paid off so many times, not just with that person but with all the people who've come into contact with him inside and outside that Best Buy store.*

> *That shows what a great leader Brian Dunn is. He's tough, he's fair, he's giving. You know, you can't be successful and have someone who continually underperforms the reasonable or realistic numbers. That's not what success looks like. So accountability is not a soft thing. You have to be willing to look in the eyes of people you like, and in many cases love, and say, "I am not happy with your performance." And be willing to say, "My job is to help you be successful." That's hard work.*

Sometimes, of course, employees just can't make the grade and have to be let go. Ron Boire and the other sales leaders we interviewed pulled no punches in addressing that fact, implicitly if not explicitly agreeing with the head of sales who remarked, "Hire slow, fire quick."

With that in mind, let's look at how the most successful sales organizations handle performance management.

# Performance Management

In keeping with their emphasis on coaching and empowering salespeople as the best way to achieve consistent high performance, the senior sales leaders we interviewed all agreed, as SAP Business Objects' Greg Lorden put it, that "the very core of sales effectiveness is management by activity rather than management by short-term results."

For one thing, the numbers alone can be deceiving. In chapter 1, "Lead from the Front," we saw that Oracle's Keith Block and other sales leaders stressed that one of the most important reasons for getting into the field is to go beyond the numbers to find out what sales reps are actually doing. A rep may be putting up great numbers with what Block called "slash-and-burn techniques" that harm customer relationships for the long term, or the numbers, good or bad, may be attributable to other factors.

Genzyme Renal's Dan Regan observed, for example, how differences in sales territories can make for distorted comparisons between equally competent sales reps. There's an interesting nuance here, in that it may be appropriate, based on differences in their territories, for two sales reps to have different activity mixes. Management by activity has a qualitative as well as a quantitative aspect.

To illustrate the value of management by activity, Greg Lorden shared two anecdotes. The first, from his time as a regional sales director, concerned a rep whose desk was right outside his office. Because he kept his door open as much as possible, Lorden regularly heard the rep on the phone with customers and prospective customers as well as internal colleagues. Lorden recounted:

> One day the rep walked into my office and said, "It's been three quarters and I haven't made my number. Should I be looking for work?"
>
> I said, "Bob, I hear you on the phone. Not only are you working hard, you're doing the right things. When you're doing the right things, I'll ride with you forever. As long as you're growing and

*learning. If you're making the same mistakes over and over again, that's a different story, but I hear you going through this. So if you're in, I'm in."*

It is important to note that Lorden had already discussed the situation with the rep's front-line sales manager and that the two of them were "in sync." That proactive alignment enabled Lorden to follow up with a note to the rep, "without going around anybody," reaffirming support for his efforts. Telling the rep, "You're going to be a great success story, if you're ready to do the extra work to get there," Lorden counseled him to work closely with the front-line manager and promised to add his own input. The result of patience and encouragement for a rep whose activity was basically on track was that:

*Last year, he was the first sales rep to qualify for [the] President's Club, and this year he was promoted to associate sales director (ASD). A guy that we almost lost is a superstar, and he's a loyal superstar because he had the right tendencies and we reinforced them.*

Lorden's second anecdote gave us the flip side of the "tough love" we mentioned at the start of this chapter. In this case, a high-performing ASD's activity had gone a little off track. Leading from the front, Lorden spent three days with the ASD and his team over the course of two weeks. He then told the ASD, "I don't see enough intensity and I don't see enough ownership." He followed this up with a note to the same effect, because "a lot of times people don't want to hear the truth, that's why you write things down." This example illustrates how, as Genzyme Renal's Dan Regan told us:

*You have to treat people with respect. You have to coach them as they should be coached. But you also have to have a backbone and let people know where they need to improve. You have to have those hard conversations where you identify an issue and address it early. Call it managerial courage.*

Or in the words of Sony's Ken Stevens, quoted above, "Sometimes you have to, in a respectful way, deliver a well-intentioned kick in the butt."

\* \* \*

No discussion of sales performance management would be complete without considering reward and recognition. For the most part, what successful sales organizations do in this regard is not surprising. What is noteworthy is the rigor with which they follow well-established principles.

They align compensation with strategic goals. They know that recognition is powerful and benefits from a sense of fun and camaraderie. They understand that everyone has a mix of motivations and that the company must be sensitive to individual differences in order to build and sustain morale.

As Cisco's Rob Lloyd said, "Compensation will get in the way unless you really pay attention to it." When Sony Electronics shifted from a sell-in sales model, in which the only goal was to pack retailers' warehouses, to a sell-through model, in which lean-inventory asset management improved business for both Sony and retailers (see chapter 4, "Advance the Science of Sales and the Art of the Customer Relationship, Part 2"), the sales organization "committed heresy," in Ken Stevens's words, "by starting to pay salespeople on supply-chain metrics, not just on sales metrics. Many people in the organization had 50 percent of their variable compensation tied to supply-chain asset management."

Aligning compensation is not a purely internal matter. It is naturally affected by the state of the human resource market for salespeople, especially competitors' compensation structures and levels, and it can also be made more complicated by macroeconomic conditions. The companies we highlight generally operated well, relative to competition, in the global downturn that began in 2007–2008, but they were hardly immune to its impact.

FedEx's Dave Edmonds described his sales organization's performance during this time as "outstanding," with continuing gains in market share, higher yields, growth in new business, and customer attrition at "an all-time low." For all that success, however, the company's base business was down simply because package volume was down throughout the economy.

Edmonds explained:

> *Therein lies a challenge with the sales force, because even though they are bringing in a lot of new business, the base business is contracting because of this whole global economic challenge that we have all been facing. They have not had as much leverage in the variable comp plans as in the past, during better economic conditions.*

*So our biggest effort has been to keep people motivated and keep their heads in the game while they are having a down year from a personal economic standpoint. There are two sides to the coin. We are doing well. We have good velocity. We have very solid, strong performance, but our people are not being compensated for the kind of work that they are doing because their base customers are contracting. It is not a loss of market share. It is not attrition to a competitor. It is just the result of the economy.*

*The challenge has been to make sure that we continue to motivate and reward in other ways where possible, and create an expectation of continued high performance."*

With regard to rewarding salespeople in other ways besides financially, senior sales leaders agreed that, in one executive's words, "hanging on to good people is not as simple as paying them gobs of money." Rather than being exclusively "coin operated," the best salespeople stay in a company because of the total direct and indirect benefits their jobs provide (see chapter 6, "Live the Mission").

From Xerox, one of the first companies to establish a "President's Club" for the best-performing sales reps, to Honeywell Building Solutions, to FedEx, sales leaders consistently boasted about their "world-class" recognition events and celebrations. Having heard about the wonderful resorts and other locations, in the United States and elsewhere, to which these sales organizations take their star salespeople, we can only say that "world-class" is no exaggeration.

Recognition need not always have a financial component. "Even the most coin-operated" salespeople, as Oracle's Keith Block described them, want to make a positive impact with their peers and customers. Accordingly, these organizations ensure that good work is recognized and praised on a regular basis via internal communications such as quarterly all-hands sales calls.

An exotic setting is not a necessity. And although appropriate financial compensation is a must, an inexpensive novelty item may be as effective a morale booster as a big-ticket item. Greg Lorden of SAP Business Objects said, "You've got to find ways for the sales force to laugh and have fun together."

Reward and recognition can be considered under the general heading of morale. You can't quantify morale. But every sales leader knows that when morale is high, sales are better.

Genzyme's Dan Regan told us:

> *Everybody's motivated by something different. Most salespeople love to see their name at the top of a list. Some are primarily motivated by money. For others it's all about the thrill of the kill, and knowing that, "Hey, I'm going to go out there and I'm going to change the perception, and I'm going to change the behaviors, and I'm going to see results."*
>
> *It's incumbent upon the front-line manager to know what makes each of the people tick."*

A final important element of reward and recognition is the career path of salespeople. For some salespeople, career development may mean a transition into sales management, marketing, or other functions. But some very good salespeople prefer to remain full-time sellers. To address this issue, FedEx and Genzyme, among other high-performing sales organizations, have created higher-level sales roles. Genzyme's Joe Brennan told us:

> *The field said they want some kind of career progression, some kind of "what is next for me" even if they want to be a professional sales rep. So we just instituted tiering, with different job titles, levels, and expectations.*

Good reward and recognition practices — indeed, all good HR practices — show the power of treating people as individuals. Sales reps may all share the same job description, but just as every territory or set of customers has its idiosyncrasies, so every effective sales rep has a distinctive personal style and individual needs and goals. Great sales organizations devote as much effort, and much the same skills, to understanding their people, as they do to understanding their customers. Only by knowing the sales organization at a fine-grained level can sales leaders meld their people's individual goals and aspirations into fulfilling the company's core goal of serving customer needs.

\* \* \*

Effective performance management requires open, two-way communication between sales leaders and the sales force. Because we have already discussed the necessity for this kind of communication in connection with collaborative leadership (see chapter 1, "Lead from the Front"), we will just give one example here, shared with us by Genzyme Renal's Dan Regan. This example illustrates why open communication within a sales organization is so important, but also suggests some ways in which sales organizations can improve. Regan said:

> *A few years ago, we did a survey that revealed we didn't have as much trust within the organization as we should. One of the things we heard is that at times people did not feel they could express their points of view without fear of ramification. That bothered me a lot.*

Regan and his leadership team responded to this unexpected result by forming a sales and marketing advisory council. Meeting in person twice a year and on conference calls every month, the rotating council membership comprises senior sales reps, product managers, and directors. "It is not a senior sales management meeting, and we do not have a lot of sales managers in there," Regan said. "It is just, 'You guys go in there, close the doors, and discuss the good and bad.'"

Regan also decided to hold "town-hall" style Q&A's at sales meetings, beginning with a national sales conference. The acid test came quickly:

> *One of our best sales reps, a great guy, stood up and said, "Dan, I don't think we're maximizing how effective we can be the way we're organized. I am not able to, and I know a lot of my colleagues are not able to, get to product three and product four. Have we ever considered or would you consider a different design?"*
>
> *Before I answered the question — I'm not telling you this story to pat myself on the back, but I think it was an important moment — I said, "Everybody hear how Dennis just asked that question? That is allowed and that's encouraged. He did it in a very professional way. He's pointing out an opportunity for us to improve as an organization, and you can feel comfortable doing that here."*
>
> *After I answered Dennis's question, I told him that his car was waiting and he could go, and that got a good laugh from everybody*

*and kind of sealed the deal that, "Wow, all right, he's not going to get fired."*

*There has to be genuine trust. It can't just be bullshit. People see through bullshit.*

Building that trust begins with "treating the sales reps with respect." Regan continued:

*You tell them, "Look, you are the most important part of the organization, not me. I am a cost center. You are the person that is out there doing it on a day-to-day basis."*

*You tell them, "I have been there. I know what it is like to be rained on, I know what it is like to step out of the car into a puddle of slush, and I know what it is like to have a door closed in your face. But you have to brush it off, you have to go back in there and make that next call."*

*So it is really believing in them and helping them believe in themselves. But if you say it and you don't believe it, they will see from your actions that you do not really mean it. You have to celebrate their victories and show them compassion during their difficult times. You have to listen to them and believe in them, and make sure you have a management team that believes in them as well.*

Formal channels for communication with the sales force must be paired with informal channels. In remarks that were consistently echoed many times in our interviews, Dan Regan spoke of the need to instill a sense that "we are all in this together, and if you have a problem or an idea, shout it out." Likewise, Joe Brennan, head of sales at Genzyme Biosurgery, said, "We constantly ask for feedback. To be a world-class organization, we need to know what is wrong and what is thought highly of in the field."

To get the sales reps to speak freely, Regan added:

*The idea of transparency goes a long way. We take some risks with our transparency. We communicate a lot more than many companies would, but we let people know that from a competitive point of view we certainly wouldn't want this out in the community.*

*You do not see that at every company. A lot of companies will tell you just what you need to know. Here there is a presumption of good will and hey, I hired you for a reason and I trust you. I think if you understand that you are building a cathedral rather than just putting bricks on the wall, you are going to do a lot more for me.*

*And I am going to do a lot more for you, and so I want you to appreciate what we are doing here and I want you to see the master plan.*

* * *

A word on attrition and turnover. This is one area where we found considerable variation among top sales organizations. Some, like Oracle as we saw in chapter 1, "Lead from the Front," are happy with around 20 percent planned annual attrition and turnover. Others believe that 20 percent is too high for excellence continuity, and prefer attrition rates of 12–15 percent. A small number of our interviewee's sales organizations have attrition rates as low as 4–5 percent. Some of these organizations focus heavily on the long-term efficiency of "highly selective hiring" and developing a very experienced sales force. Others in this group are concerned that very low attrition implies that they are not moving out enough low performers.

The economic downturn beginning in 2007–2008 forced all these organizations to reassess their attrition rates, and in some cases to increase them as a cost-cutting necessity. Despite this macroeconomic pressure, however, there was general agreement that repeated attrition rates much higher than 20 percent likely indicate an unhealthy sales organization.

## Conclusion

The most successful sales organizations are convinced, and act on their conviction day-by-day, that, as Ken Stevens of Sony Electronics told us:

*If you create an environment where you show people that they are empowered to make decisions, both in terms of authority and responsibility, that you marry the two of those together, people have a tendency to want to do well, not just for themselves, but for you. When you give them the tools, then they say, "You have trusted me in this environment. You have armed me. You have made it my call. Now you're holding me accountable for it, and I'm not letting you down."*

Based on our interviews and other research, we have no doubt that speaking clearly — and carrying a big carrot — will indeed raise the bar on sales organization accountability and excellence.

**HOW GREAT SALES ORGANIZATIONS FOSTER GREAT INDIVIDUAL AND TEAM PERFORMANCE BY SPEAKING CLEARLY — AND CARRYING A BIG CARROT**

- Make hiring and training a consistent priority.
- Treat HR expenditures as an investment in the sales organization's, and the entire firm's, future.
- View selling as a training ground for general management, as well as sales management.
- Manage the sales force by activity, not only by results.
- Devote substantial effort and ingenuity to reward and recognition programs that align financial incentives with satisfying customer needs and inspire a commitment to sales excellence.
- Deal with the sales force in a spirit of tough love, supporting and empowering salespeople in combination with clear expectations, limits, and scorecards.

# CHAPTER 3

# Advance the Science of Sales and the Art of the Customer Relationship, Part 1

**IN THE FIRST TWO CHAPTERS OF THIS BOOK** we have looked at sales excellence in terms of a sales organization's leadership and HR practices, always with an eye on the increasing complexity of sales roles. In this and the following chapter we consider organizational sales excellence and individual sales roles in terms of the sales process itself.

As we studied high-performing sales organizations across industries and markets, we saw them making their sales processes ever more scientific (more predictable, more reliable, and more robust), while also deepening and strengthening customer relationships. These sales organizations excel at:

- Fact-based decision making that keeps the human element in mind and never loses sight of customer needs.

- Focused, flexible resource allocation across customer segments and sales channels.

- Matching sales models, including the mix of channels and of generalist and specialist sales roles, to evolving customer needs.

- Leveraging increasingly sophisticated intellectual capital in roles where an old-style generalist seller's responsibility would have been largely confined to relationship management.

- Continuous improvement of sales analytics, sales processes, and sales operations.

- Alignment of individual and organizational performance measures.

\* \* \*

Sales executives frequently spoke to us about "the science of sales" in contrast to longstanding notions of sales as a catch basin for people without the intellectual ability to perform well in other functions. David Smith, from J&J's Vistakon subsidiary, summed it up this way:

*Sales has typically been considered kind of the red-haired stepchild in terms of business sophistication. But there is a real appreciation here for the importance of sales, and an understanding that there is a science to it and that it can be managed in a fact-based, data-driven fashion. It is just as sophisticated as any other functionality, and you can develop some great general business managers out of the sales function.*

We explore the science of sales mainly through the operations and achievements of three high-performing sales organizations, ranging from "new tech" to "old tech" and back again: Hewlett-Packard (HP), Whirlpool, and Sony Electronics. Among other things, the juxtaposition of these companies shows the shakiness of such labels as "old tech" and "new tech," given the pace of technology development throughout the economy and how demanding sales roles have become across the entire business landscape. We also take up the related question of whether there is still a need for generalist salespeople — this was the one major issue where we found apparent disagreement among the most successful sales organizations — and we examine the rigorous sales process at Honeywell Building Solutions.

Part of the new science of sales has come through increasing sophistication in sales operations infrastructure and support. At HP, among other firms, sales operations designs and implements a monitor and control system for the sales organization. Modern sales operations teams perform analytical functions that streamline and power pipeline management in terms of such activities as lead generation, automation of request for proposal and contract processes, and development and implementation of new field sales tools. Sales operations may also have responsibility for sales force and front-line sales management training. This is the case, for example, at both HP and FedEx (for this aspect of FedEx sales operations, see chapter 2, "Speak Clearly — and Carry a Big Carrot").

The consistently outstanding results achieved by the sales organizations of HP, Whirlpool, and Sony Electronics, among others, fully validate *the science of sales*, or as HP's Andy Mattes put it, "taking sales from an art to a science." However, in the spirit of what's old is new again, this is in large part because advancing the science of sales has become the best means of renewing the art of managing the customer relationship. Elite sales organizations have engineered a feedback loop in which creative, empowered, highly skilled salespeople deploy rigorous sales processes to do consultative selling as customers' trusted business partners. Once again J&J/Vistakon's David Smith could have been speaking for all the sales leaders we interviewed when he said:

> *All sales are relationship driven. On the one hand, your ability to develop relationships and establish credibility with customers depends on being able to make a technically compelling case for the solutions you bring. But on the other hand, you can't make the case well without a really deep identification with, and empathy for, the customer.*

As we shall see, great sales organizations work every day to align the science of sales with the art of the customer relationship, balancing the quantitative and qualitative, the objective and subjective, sides of the sales function.

## *Taking Sales from an Art to a Science at Hewlett-Packard*

The R&D and business systems originally established at Hewlett-Packard (HP) by William Hewlett and David Packard drove enormous growth long after its two founders stepped aside from day-to-day management. It also drove a generalist sales model that successfully adapted to HP's expansion from precision instrumentation into computers, printing and imaging, and software.

As the global IT industry matured, however, time eroded the advantages of this "product-out" model represented by generalist sellers. To keep designing and developing relevant products and services, HP, along with competing IT firms, had to adopt a "customer-in" model relying on increasing numbers of specialist salespeople.

For a time, the prevailing wisdom within the IT world was that customers would do their own aggregating and coordinating of the specialized products and services their businesses required. In fact, they also wanted help in this area, help that new teams of specialists and a new breed of generalist seller would have to provide. Louis V. Gerstner famously brought IBM back from the brink with his early recognition of this market reality, which drove his transformation of IBM from mainly a computer mainframe manufacturer to a provider of comprehensive hardware and software products and services.

IBM could not long remain the only player of this game, however. Over the past several years, HP has shrewdly positioned itself as a market share and profit leader in the IT industry worldwide by providing a complete spectrum of products and services. Among the most significant of its recent moves has been to expand its portfolio with the multi-billion dollar acquisition of systems integrator EDS.

In extended conversations at corporate headquarters in Palo Alto, CA, Andy Mattes, senior vice president at HP's EDS Americas division, and his colleague Olivier Kohler, senior vice president of HP's Global Alliances Technology Solutions, gave us insight into how HP has achieved these results and positioned itself for continuing future growth and profitability. Their operating premise, Andy Mattes said, is that "sales is the science of creating shareholder value."

\* \* \*

On joining HP, Andy Mattes found "pockets of brilliance," but "a lack of systematic underpinnings," in the sales organization. The generalist sales force was a legacy from the time when, Olivier Kohler said:

> *The products carried themselves. The value proposition was, "These are great products." That's why we had generalist salespeople. For a long period, if you were a generalist and you could represent the same layer of many, many things, you were well appreciated.*

No company's products can carry themselves in the 21st century IT industry, because competitors also offer good products and services at attractive prices. Andy Mattes therefore beat the drum on "taking sales from an art to a science," precisely in order to further the art of the customer relationship. He elaborated:

> *You need sales executives who add value to the customer. So I have been driving very hard to get away from generalist models. I don't believe in generalists. You are either an expert in a client, or you are an expert in a vertical, or you are an expert in a solution, or you are an expert in a technology. But you've got to be an expert in something. Just to be the chief executive coffee drinker won't hack*

*it anymore. You will either blow it on the effectiveness, or you will blow it on the cost side.*

*Be an expert in one area. With a product portfolio as large as ours, you can never understand it all. But if you hold your own through two or three rounds of conversation in one area, it enhances your credibility. When you then say, "I am sure about this, but I am not sure about that. Let me ask my colleague to join us, because he or she is the resident expert on that," you are still in the picture. You are being valued as somebody who knows what he or she is good at and where his or her borders are.*

*If you can't hold your own in one area, you don't get a second or third meeting.*

Speaking to the same point, Olivier Kohler noted that the key to "creating distinctiveness" in HP's offerings is "the way you wrap things together." For example, an enterprise systems solution may include software, servers, data center monitoring, and a plan for outsourcing. "We lead the conversation from a customer business requirement rather than the product. That has required skill change in the sales force, which is still going on."

Andy Mattes established a framework for developing a specialist sales model by asking "a few very simple questions." HP needed clarity on existing and potential customers, how the sales force matched up with them, and any gaps in coverage. "We were pretty rigorous in conjugating this thing down," Mattes said, "and we noticed we did not even cover some of what we call the G2K, the global 2000 largest IT spenders." A closer look revealed that although HP ostensibly had a strategic account management structure, "many very attractive targets were covered by salespeople who had 10, 15, or even 20 'strategic' accounts. Well, there's an oxymoron. That's not consultative selling; that's drive-by shooting."

HP's sales leadership saw potential for specialist sellers in a "high-density coverage model." Andy Mattes explained:

*There is a very simple inverse correlation. If I charter you as a sales person to cover fifteen or twenty accounts, you have no choice but to swing by the procurement offices and ask, "Is there a bid for me?" You have to go to the lowest guy at the customer's organization by default.*

*The fewer accounts you have to cover, the more time you have to work your way up in the customer's organization. You can think about your customer's business and get more proactive. You can start having more intelligent conversations.*

*One of our basic findings was that our coverage model could set the sales organization up for success, or set them up for failure and inefficiency. So we dramatically reduced the number of accounts per seller. We took people with 20 mid-sized accounts down to five or six, and people with five or six big accounts down to one or two strategic accounts.*

Cutting the number of accounts per sales person meant adding hundreds of people to the direct sales force, and HP's channel organization "initially got very worried that this would be anti-channel." The results proved otherwise. On the accounts where HP made the change, it "more than doubled pipeline growth" and "channel business went up," Andy Mattes said, because "if somebody is creating mind share for HP, it's not only good for HP, it's good for the overall HP ecosystem." The channel organization's enthusiasm for the new high-density sales model became "one of the biggest wins we've had."

At the time of our conversation, HP had 12,000 salespeople around the world, and Andy Mattes wryly observed, "Scale makes you nimble." Seeing the surprise this comment evoked, Mattes said:

*Think about it this way. For a company the size of Hewlett-Packard, the next half-billion-dollar deal, the next billion-dollar deal, as big as it is, does not solve our growth challenge. Winning the next big deal is an important thing; it's not the answer. But the quota for every one of my 12,000 salespeople is anywhere between three and six million bucks. If on average we can drive the quota achievement per sales person up 10 percent, times 12,000 — start doing the math, and you see it's a huge lever.*

*When you work big numbers, you have to enable a big organization to grow. And it is thousands of wins that get you there. That's the big picture. That's why I say scale makes you nimble. Because I don't care who you are in the organization, you can't do it by yourself.*

A sales organization can only secure thousands of wins if it has the "systematic underpinnings" that were missing when Andy Mattes joined HP. He and his fellow sales leaders have accordingly taken enormous pains to hone the company's sales operations support and service competencies. At HP, sales operations functions as a flexible interface between sales and marketing, as an engineering house for global sales and support processes, and as an agent of both continuous improvement and transformational change.

# Is the Generalist Sales Person Obsolete?

The turn to specialist sales roles at HP parallels that at Oracle and reflects a strong trend within the IT industry. Although sales roles are becoming more and more specialized throughout the B2B world, this does not mean that the generalist seller has gone the way of the dodo bird. As Mark Twain cabled from London after American newspapers had printed his obituary, "The reports of my death are greatly exaggerated."

Current and future sales challenges do not call for killing off generalist sellers. Rather, they call for repositioning the generalist seller with value beyond relationship maintenance. This in turn calls for reprovisioning the generalist seller with new forms of intellectual capital. In this regard, we can observe that it is not so much that the generalist sales role has become obsolete as that the route to a generalist role and the level at which it can most commonly be effective have changed.

To put this in terms of sales career paths, where the generalist role could once be both an entry-level and career-long job, or something a seller transitioned out of to take on a specialist role, in a growing number of industries today it is more often the case that a specialist seller ascends to a generalist role in key account management. As a generational shift in sales management occurs with the retirements of the remaining cohorts of Baby Boomers, this trend will continue. More and more sales leaders will have spent the early and middle part of their careers in specialist, rather than generalist, sales roles.

Key account management almost inevitably dictates a continuing role for high-caliber generalist salespeople, however. The larger and more complex the customer, the more a sales organization needs people who can look across both the customer's requirements and the selling firm's capabilities to craft and manage the delivery of complex value propositions.

Both HP and Oracle implicitly acknowledge this. Note how HP's Andy Mattes characterizes being "an expert in one area," not as sufficient for all purposes but as something that "enhances your credibility" in complex situations: "… if you hold your own through two or three rounds of conversation in one area, … you [can] then say, '… Let me ask my colleague to join us, because he or she is the resident expert on that,' … . If you can't hold your own in one area, you don't get a second or third meeting." These comments map a transition from playing a specialist sales role alone to leading, or co-leading, a team of fellow specialists.

Oracle's Keith Block similarly observed that with some particularly complex customers, his sales organization adjusts its specialist-only approach by designating one of the specialists as a key account director (see chapter 1, "Lead from the Front"). At the highest echelon of Oracle's sales organization, sales executives such as Block himself play a sophisticated generalist role, leading Oracle specialists in close engagement with the firm's most important customers.

The value of a broad perspective in strategic account management lies behind the description in many sales organizations of the key account manager, or key account director, as a quarterback. Cisco, FedEx, and Xerox, among others, deploy sales quarterbacks effectively at the head of cross-functional sales teams.

On balance it seems to us that the most successful sales organizations differ more in rhetoric than substance on the question of specialists versus generalists. Certainly the days are gone when generalist account managers could survive on people skills alone. No matter what the industry, sealing the deal now requires technological and/or business sophistication far beyond the level that was once sufficient. But by the same token the sales leader tasked with coordinating the fulfillment of complex customer requirements cannot command specialist sales knowledge in every area. The sales leader must instead have the intellectual capital to guide the conversation between specialists on both sides of the deal.

## The Emerging Relationship between Sales and Marketing: A Partnership of Peers

Sales leaders and the sales organization as a whole must also have the intellectual capital for a new kind of internal conversation. The sales organization must be able to engage the marketing organization in a cooperative dialogue that reflects and furthers their evolving responsibilities and the evolving balance between them.

Once upon a time, marketing fulfilled the role of architect and sales served as a contractor, or in many firms a subcontractor. Without taking anything away from marketing's business-wide responsibilities, this division of labor will no longer do the job. In high-performing firms the sales and marketing organizations are building a new relationship, a partnership of peers. This trend is among the most important recent developments in advancing the science of sales and the art of the customer relationship.

To appreciate the magnitude of the trend, consider the relative roles of marketing and sales as described in a typical business school marketing textbook:

> *Marketing: Determines the needs and wants of target markets and adapts the organization to delivering desirable products/services more effectively and efficiently than the competition.*
>
> *Sales: Designed around the assumption that customers will not buy a product or service unless a significant effort is made to stimulate interest and need.*

In other words marketing, done right, minimizes the need for a sales function. And sellers mainly push products that as a result of weak marketing don't "sell themselves." If this were ever true, it no longer describes the world of B2B marketing and sales. The role of B2B sales has evolved well beyond "product pusher" to encompass value creation and delivery not even contemplated in the definitions above.

We documented the following responsibilities for the sales organization in a typical high-growth B2B company:

- Works with customers to identify and articulate their business needs
- Supplements company products with advisory services designed to offer customers solutions to their business needs
- Partners with the marketing organization to identify specific customer segments that have like issues and needs for particular solutions
- Partners with the marketing organization to develop repeatable services and tools to more efficiently and effectively deliver solutions to customers
- Builds specialist expertise in particular industries and product and service areas to fashion and deliver business solutions to customer issues

- Works with specialists (often funded by the marketing organization) to install and implement solutions for customers

- Works with customers to refine installed solutions, identify opportunities for additional solutions, and provide unvarnished feedback to the marketing organization

Instead of looking at customers through the lens of product features, sales and marketing team up to create and deliver value by designing offerings in the context of evolving customer needs. Far from pushing unwanted products, 21st century sellers manage their intellectual capital, as marketers manage theirs, to identify business problems and deliver solutions that enable customers to increase revenues, decrease costs, or both.

The classic marketing to sales "hand-off" no longer adequately describes this complex relationship or the close cooperation it requires. The relationship is instead best pictured as a series of loops (see diagram) in which marketing and sales repeatedly interact, with sales primarily focused on creating value for the customer and marketing focused on creating value for BOTH the customer and sales.

In this model, marketing and sales have a symbiotic relationship and a shared responsibility to enhance their company's market position, market share, revenue growth, and profit. The classic analogy of marketing as the architect and sales as the contractor has given way to a new paradigm wherein both functions serve, and work together, as "design–build" architects.

HP is one of the high-performing organizations in which this new paradigm is taking hold and creating significant customer value. It advances the science of sales by making sales processes more reliable, predictable, and repeatable. At the same time, it advances the art of the customer relationship by deepening sales and marketing organizations' shared understanding of customer needs. The result is enriched value for customers, and enhanced customer loyalty for the firms savvy enough to embrace and exploit the power of partnership between sales and marketing.

In HP's case, as we shall see, the engine for transforming the relationship between sales and marketing is sales operations. Still relatively new and marginal in many firms, sales operations gathers and analyzes both internal and external data. In leading-edge sales organizations like HP and J&J's eye-care subsidiary Vistakon (see chapter 6, "Live the Mission"), sales operations has become a vital link to field marketing, itself a new phenomenon, and constitutes the next wave in customer understanding and engage-

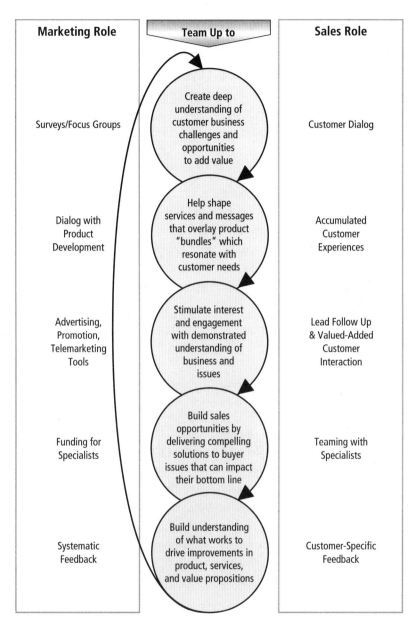

| Marketing Role | Team Up to | Sales Role |
| --- | --- | --- |
| Surveys/Focus Groups | Create deep understanding of customer business challenges and opportunities to add value | Customer Dialog |
| Dialog with Product Development | Help shape services and messages that overlay product "bundles" which resonate with customer needs | Accumulated Customer Experiences |
| Advertising, Promotion, Telemarketing Tools | Stimulate interest and engagement with demonstrated understanding of business and issues | Lead Follow Up & Valued-Added Customer Interaction |
| Funding for Specialists | Build sales opportunities by delivering compelling solutions to buyer issues that can impact their bottom line | Teaming with Specialists |
| Systematic Feedback | Build understanding of what works to drive improvements in product, services, and value propositions | Customer-Specific Feedback |

ment. Sometimes housed within the marketing organization and sometimes within the sales organization, but always working hand-in-hand with field sales, field marketing takes sales operations data and creates powerful new sales tools. In taking the lead in field marketing, high-performing companies are truly taking the science of sales and the art of the customer relationship into the future.

# The Sales Operations Interface between Sales and Marketing at HP

Addressing the interaction between sales and marketing, Olivier Kohler observed that there is a perhaps inevitable tension between "their different viewpoints." In HP's case, its history as a "product-out company with very strong product marketing" did not prepare it well to help specialist salespeople represent products and services in terms of customer solutions rather than technical features.

"The change in the sales force from a large pool of generalists to a pool of specialists," Kohler said, "means you need to target information for the roles that salespeople are playing." From telesales to farmers and hunters to "client business managers with one strategic account" to industry specialists with expertise in areas such as financial systems integration, different salespeople need to access and deploy widely varied knowledge sets.

HP sales operations has met this challenge by creating a central portal for a company-wide sales knowledge base. Sales operations draws content from both R&D and product marketing, and then shapes and segments it for both particular sales roles and particular steps in the sales process, from opportunity to lead to bid to close. Olivier Kohler explained:

> It is easy to segment content by product; it is a little more compli-
> cated to do it by role. Putting the content into the context of who
> you are as a sales person and how the sales process works creates a
> different set of challenges for content management. We work with
> the people creating the products and the people in marketing, and
> then we take their information and work in the middle to do the
> magic to say, "Okay, product marketers, the information is great.
> But salespeople need to have that translated in relation to the solu-
> tions they are selling, which is slightly different." It creates what we
> call a "Smart Flow" of knowledge for the sales force.

The "Smart Flow" knowledge base for all of HP's products and services counters the tendency for every product line to be marketed like "the king of the hill." It also facilitates solution selling by enabling sales operations to configure the "nuts and bolts" of bids. Even specialist salespeople cannot know all the technical details in their areas of expertise, much less those in related parts of complex product and service packages. "You cannot ask salespeople to go to the complexity of building the products," Olivier Kohler said. "You want the salespeople to have the expertise to translate for the customers how the products work and how they can meet the customers' business requirements. We are telling them to forget about the nuts and bolts, and we will configure how the rack cable and the cooling system and the storage and the software all go together, and make the pricing work, so that we become the right arm of the salespeople."

Developing this competency in sales operations has helped spur "a big change in marketing," which has evolved to become better at "putting product marketing into the context of what the customer wants to do." Product marketing then becomes "the next layer down, the details of how HP's products and services will help solve" the customer's business requirement. At the same time, HP does not want to jettison all its "product-out DNA." As Olivier Kohler put it:

> You want to be a great product company. You want to be pushing state-of-the-art designs out into the industry. But you have to represent the customer's view, not just the product view, so that you get the best of both worlds. There was a product-out orientation, and now it's more of a customer-in orientation, and sales operations is basically in the middle enabling the transition between the two worlds, because both worlds have value-add.

In addition to different points of view on how to represent products and services, sales and marketing have different points of view on opportunity identification and lead generation, and their usefulness in pursuing and closing sales. The classic argument, Olivier Kohler noted, is when marketing says, "Here are all the opportunities and leads we give you," and sales says, "You're not giving us anything we can actually use." But if it is natural that "there is always tension" between sales and marketing, sales operations has helped HP to make this tension "constructive" and provide sales and marketing with "more common ground."

It has done so by creating a range of global sales and support processes like the "Smart Flow" knowledge base.

## Engineering Global Sales and Support Processes

"When we talk about taking sales from an art to a science," Andy Mattes told us, it is vital to provide "consistent data." He added, "The biggest change we are driving is to have end-to-end information, true end-to-end data availability and comparability." Addressing the same point, Olivier Kohler spoke of HP's need for sales operations to provide "the discipline of globally consistent processes."

The centerpiece of these efforts, which Andy Mattes called "a monster milestone within HP," has been the creation of a global sales pipeline for all of HP's products and services that reaches across 170 countries. "It took three and a half years, and it wasn't pretty," Olivier Kohler said of the pipeline's design, construction, and implementation. Instead of "every major country team doing whatever they wanted, there is now one process, one instance." HP lets country and regional teams "localize" their pipeline inputs with "different flavors," but "we do not allow customization."

HP's sales leaders manage the global pipeline in terms of shape, size, and velocity in every stage from opportunity to lead to bid to close. They can see where volume is lean or where things are getting stuck, and they can answer precise questions such as whether key accounts in the United States, for example, are leading or lagging overall performance numbers. They can monitor behavioral patterns in the sales force by country, noticing for example, Andy Mattes said, "that culturally our folks in Japan don't like to show how the deals progress. They want to keep them in the early stage, and then go straight to close." Sales operations' information enables sales management to clarify where sales teams are running into problems and where opportunities are being left on the table. It also facilitates sharing best practices throughout the sales organization.

One of the most important benefits of the global sales pipeline is that it enables like-for-like comparisons. Andy Mattes explained:

> Every time we looked at Latin America we'd get this set of numbers and 1,200 reasons why things are not comparable to the United States. And in all fairness, they aren't. All of a sudden, we can compare Latin America with Iberia, and it's like, wait a minute. Some of the key players that you are doing business with in Latin America are actually headquartered in Iberia. Now tell us why your performance is better or worse. Or we can compare Brazil with Russia, India, and China as part of the BRIC countries, versus comparing Brazil with Canada, which will give different dynamics.
>
> Transparency, good numbers, clarity—they all foster intelligent conversation and action.

HP exploits the global pipeline to set sales goals for the whole company and its three business groups (enterprise solutions; business and consumer PCs, workstations, and mobile devices; and printing and imaging), as well as for countries, regions, territories, and even individual salespeople. Andy Mattes pointed to the enterprise solutions market as an example. At the time of our first interview in 2008, the global enterprise market opportunity was roughly $500 billion and HP was reported to have roughly eight percent market share. Mattes said:

> *HP happens to be the largest IT company on the planet. Wouldn't it be reasonable for the largest IT company to have a market share north of 10 percent? If you take a bottom-up view of account plans, you will always end up with a growth number that is at or below market. And if you look at things from the 50,000 foot, top-down level, you see where you can stretch the organization. And it's between those two points where you want to have a healthy conversation about how far you want to drive the organization, about whether you want top-line focus on margin or bottom-line focus on which accounts will produce the highest yield.*

When HP is contemplating new sales investments, it uses global-pipeline data to make the business case. "What you want to look at is the ratio of gross margin over field sales costs," Mattes said. "And then you can ask yourself how much more gross margin dollars you can generate with the next dollar of field selling costs." As long as there is headroom in the total addressable market and the sales organization has not reached a point of diminishing returns, "it's not even the CEO that's driving the top line, it is the sales organization. And our yield on the next field-selling cost dollar has not gone down. Au contraire, the more we target the right opportunities, it's actually gone up. As long as we have that, we are going to keep investing."

The global sales pipeline has produced "a big conversation change," in Olivier Kohler's words, because "a sales manager, a district manager, a territory manager, a country manager, you name it, can now open the system and say, 'Hmm, this account, I am not sure the pipeline size is right,' and then pick up the phone" and go right to the relevant people to clarify the matter and discuss appropriate steps. Because the pipeline management process is the same worldwide, the CEO can instantly check "the top few deals across the world at any given time with visibility at his fingertips, [whereas previously this required] a lot of people in the background making phone calls and pulling stuff together."

At every level from global to local territory efforts, sales and marketing interaction has improved, because they can now use pipeline data to draw up ranked opportunity lists. The bottom line, Andy Mattes said, is that the global pipeline has become "a very powerful tool for challenging the organization. All of a sudden, you get an opportunity-driven, outside-in view versus an inside-out view." With a clear sense of the opportunity in the market, "your product, your solution offering, your delivery capabilities become enablers or inhibitors. But they no longer become initiators of your actions."

It is important to note that the pipeline data need not be absolutely precise but only "directionally correct." As Mattes wryly put it, "If you decide to go on a diet, it doesn't truly matter whether your bathroom scale is a hundred percent correct. If you get on the same scale every morning and you're really dieting, you'll notice the delta."

HP embraces the transparency the global sales pipeline provides and publishes it throughout the sales organization. This transparency has had a positive effect on sales force turnover and on both sales and sales management training. Andy Mattes said:

> *The transparency does two things. It drives natural attrition up. Salespeople who continually see themselves on the low end of the totem pole—they more likely come to the right conclusion before anybody else does it for them. And second, the transparency drives you into more of a coaching culture and you start having good portfolio conversations, especially with young salespeople who are learning their jobs and are not quite there yet.*

As we saw in chapter 2, "Speak Clearly — and Carry a Big Carrot," HP fosters the performance of salespeople and sales managers with rigorous "license to practice" and "license to manage" training programs run by sales operations. In addition to running sales training around the world, HP's sales operations has linked pipeline management to a set of other global sales and support processes. These processes are designed to facilitate pipeline movement from opportunity to lead to bid to close.

At the sales pipeline funnel's mouth, Olivier Kohler said, HP sellers use "Customer Intent Capture Forms [to] match the customer's intent to what we have to offer." Having "a formal framework" focuses the sales force to think critically about "the business problem the customer is trying to solve" rather than about HP's products and services on their own terms.

IT customers are not shy about telling prospective vendors what their rivals are offering. The Customer Intent Capture Forms start a process of positioning HP's solutions against those from Dell, IBM, or other players. Sales operations has the task of supporting salespeople with business intelligence that takes into account such rival offerings as well as customer buying patterns in different industry niches or parts of the world.

In a competitive bidding situation in Germany, for example, sales operations will feed the sales person information about what customers in that segment and region tend to buy. Then, as Kohler explained, "the sales person can go to the customer and say, 'Here are a couple of ideas for what you want to do. And by the way, here are the configurations that are being bought in your field and their pros and cons.'" The sales person is then positioned to have a truly consultative discussion about the best way to meet the customer's business requirement.

To advance that discussion, Kohler continued, "we have created what we call 'Express Lane' in sales operations." This is a system for drafting bid proposals that "in two days' work [delivers] a customized value proposition" complete with product configurations and pricing.

At HP, sales operations is charged to contribute to "sales leads, customer knowledge management, sales information, sales training, bid management, and contract development," Olivier Kohler said. That charge includes both achieving continuous improvement in execution and innovating ways "to shape the future of the sales organization." In terms of advancing the science of sales, this all goes to making sales processes more fact-based, reliable, and predictable. The benefit to advancing the art of the customer relationship is in the way effective sales operations frees up time for, and supports, that vital activity.

## *Continuous Improvement and Transformational Change*

Doing more with less is a familiar challenge in today's business world. Speaking to that challenge, Andy Mattes said, "At the end of the day the sales organization only has two levers for driving shareholder value. We can take costs out of the company, and we can grow." These levers are of course not an either/or proposition. All sales leaders interested in the long-term viability of their organizations must press them both as effectively as possible.

In terms of the science of sales, sales operations has become an HP "center of expertise" for both execution improvement and innovation. Its ultimate responsibility, Olivier Kohler said, is "bringing the sales force to a level that is industry leading in terms of productivity." To that end, Kohler says that in sales operations, "our product is the sales experience," for the company and its customers alike. This requires a dual focus on both "optimizing current operations [and developing] new sales experiences that will make a difference and change the game."

Kohler's sales operations staff thus does "engineering, execution, and transformation." It is structured into a "front office and a back office." The front office serves as "the right arm of sales productivity," and the back office "brings necessary efficiency for the company at large" as well as for sales.

The front office supports the sales force's transition from generalist to specialist sales and "from one-to-many to high density, one-to-a-few or one-to-one sales coverage." The back office handles "repetitive, scalable tasks" like the "Express Lane" bid configuration that we discussed above.

Kohler offered two intriguing examples of how sales operations can have a positive impact on activity in other areas of the company. In its role as the interface between sales and marketing, sales operations has helped HP's printing and imaging group create "the same product structure" in its business and consumer divisions and "save money in the supply chain." And as HP regularly buys smaller companies in software or hardware niches to bolster its solution offerings, sales operations streamlines the acquisitions process by integrating new products and services into global sales processes "within 90 days."

The ratio of front office to back office staff in sales operations varies according to broad sales force challenges and regional market variations. To support the shift to high-density sales coverage, "the front office had to be rescaled and tuned" to salespeople having a few, rather than many, accounts. And whereas "in mature markets like Western Europe, the United States, and Canada, where there is a greater amount of repetitiveness or at least things you can predict, I usually have 20/80, 20 percent in the front office and 80 percent in the back office," Kohler explained. "In fast-growing countries, where we are trying to figure out what works and what customers like, I have put a little bit more in the front office to help navigate the space."

On a quarterly basis, Kohler measures the effectiveness of the front office/back office ratios and the numbers of sales operations staff working on execution, engineering, and transformation. Every year to two years, he does "a hard assessment" to be sure that things are working well, paying particular attention to measuring *opportunity to lead to bid to close* and other performance metrics.

Selling time is an especially critical measure for HP. Echoing Woody Allen's dictum that 90 percent of life is just showing up, both Andy Mattes and Olivier Kohler said, "You sell more when you show up." To begin with, the measure was of customer-facing time, but "we were starting to get funny behavior," Kohler said, "like if you show up and have a beer with the customer, it's good. But," said Kohler, "when you show up you close, it's better." After what Kohler called "a religious debate," the measure has evolved to include "non-customer-facing" but still "value-add" time, such as time spent on account planning and proposal development, but to *exclude* "non-value add" time, even if it is spent with the customer.

One of Olivier Kohler's trickiest tasks is to balance "execution efficiency [with] transformation ability." He has delegated "a fire-drill team" to solve day-to-day problems and "a long-term team" to work on transformation issues. Kohler told us:

> *I keep talking to my organization about how we are executing and how we are transforming, and those are two different things. Execution is day-to-day metrics, don't break the machine, make it efficient. Transformation is taking risk, showing that we can change the game.*

> *What I worry about is that if we create too rigid a structure or process, our transformation ability, our adaptability, becomes lower. So we are also trying to move the ball two steps ahead of the game. And if you want to do that, you break stuff. But that's okay.*

> *If we only measure sales operations by what we bring in efficiencies, they will be as fast as the size of the wheel. You can make the wheel turn very fast, but you reach limits. Sometimes the better way is to change the size of the wheel and crank at a different rate, because*

*there is a thin line where the sales experience can be continuously improved.*

*Or an analogy we use is that you can become like a hamster running in a wheel. The hamster can run as fast as he wants, and he won't go anywhere.*

*So we have day-to-day metrics to manage a cadence of improvements, and longer-term metrics to manage a cadence of transformation.*

*But we should never be naïve. We have to execute. If you don't execute well, it's hard to transform."*

The shift to a global sales pipeline exemplifies the need to "drive change with a really strong fist for a while" in order to overcome an organization's inevitable "passive resistance." We've already considered HP's global pipeline as a sales process. But in terms of organizational change, it is also important to recognize that HP's sales leaders had to marshal the combined force of sales operations, sales management buy-in, and new compensation incentives before the sales organization would accept the global pipeline and adjust its behavior to exploit it. Kohler explained:

*To change the sales force's behavior — and this is where sales operations doesn't get popular, but it's necessary — we said that if the sale wasn't in the pipeline, there was no comp. Then we needed sales management to embrace it and say they would not look at a forecast if it wasn't in the pipeline.*

*Before the global pipeline, we had a central repository, but the salespeople were constantly explaining why their numbers weren't in there or why they were different from what we thought.*

*We told them, "We don't want to hear why your number is different. Tell us what it will take to be equal." And the next step after that was, "You don't need to tell us why it's different, because there is only one place we will look at it."*

*Now that there is only one place to look, the salespeople don't waste time justifying their own numbers. They spend time fixing the number in the pipeline. It sounds so simple, but for a big sales organization it is so major.*

*The shift to a global pipeline was very threatening, because sales-people's value-add is what they have in their heads, the individual way they operate. So it's not very comfortable for them to have to lay out everything and estimate things they are not sure of. Their mind-set was, "I know my account. My data is better. And by the way, my data is either in my head, in my spreadsheet, or in my laptop." But it wasn't anywhere sales management could see it and discuss it with them.*

*Now we have changed the conversation. We say, "As a sales rep or an account manager, you still know the account better than anybody else. But you have to make that visible to the rest of the organization."*

# Conclusion

Summing up the responsibilities for the science of sales, from day-to-day metrics to process innovation, that HP has entrusted to sales operations, Olivier Kohler said:

*I fundamentally believe sales operations can be a change agent for the company. Most companies say sales operations is the tactical arm. That's good, but is it good enough?*

*HP has given sales operations an opportunity to change the game, and that means both execution and transformation. The way I have said it to my organization is, "If you do execution well, you earn the right to be at the table for the transformation. If you mess up the execution, you lose your right to be at the transformation table."*

*We want to be at the transformation table, because that is a little bit more intellectually challenging. But that's something you earn. It doesn't come for free.*

These dual roles have "energized" the sales operations workforce, Kohler added, "and an energized workforce means better results. [Through] a lot of hard work — you can call it internal marketing — we have positioned the sales operations organization to be perceived and valued differently based on tangible results." Sales operations is no longer "a grinding machine measured only on efficiencies."

Not content with what sales operations has accomplished to date, Olivier Kohler envisions a "self-sufficient, self-service" sales force that will require sales operations to evolve in new ways and to become even more of a standard bearer for using science and technology to enhance the sales organization's relationships with customers. He said:

> *Today I have too many people helping sales, because we don't yet provide good enough self-sufficiency for the sales force. Many companies patch things up with sales operations. In my opinion, that's not the right model. The model is the self-help check-in at the airport and things like that. We hated it when it showed up, but guess what? It works.*
>
> *Where I want to bring the sales force is to arm them to be dangerous with mobile tools for bid configuration and bid management. But it cannot be to the detriment of their productivity, and that is the big challenge.*

HP has a multi-year program "to change the game with self-sufficiency" via mobile tools. It will be fascinating to see how this develops over time. Now let's move to chapter 4 and see how other leading sales organizations are advancing the science of sales and the art of the customer relationship.

# CHAPTER 4

# Advance the Science of Sales and the Art of the Customer Relationship, Part 2

**HP IS BY NO MEANS ALONE** in establishing and constantly refining rigorous sales processes. Many other firms have also devoted themselves to turning sales into a science in this way. For example, the remarkable turnaround at Honeywell Building Solutions (HBS) in the 2000s entailed a rededication to sophisticated sales pipeline management after the firm temporarily lost focus in this area. Like HP, HBS refined its approach to the science of the sales process in order to renew its mastery of the art of the customer relationship.

HBS organizes its sales efforts, from lead to close, through an activity and decision matrix it calls the Breakaway Sales Process. The process has five steps, and each step has several points or components that together contribute to an outcome that determines whether or not the process advances to the next step. Steps one to three comprise the preparatory phase of the sales process: Step four is the "breakaway" phase, where HBS strives to secure differential advantage over the competition in the customer's eyes. Step five finalizes the agreement with the customer.

Within each of its five steps, the HBS Sales Process clearly defines a business purpose, sets of key tasks, tools, and enablers, a go/no-go decision point, and a desired outcome. Thus step one, making the first calls on a promising lead, has the business purpose of discovering the customer's needs and the potential value in the deal for both the customer and HBS. The decision HBS makes here is one of qualification: Should it compete for the business, and can it deliver value on both sides of the deal? The desired outcome is a decision schedule signed by both the customer and HBS. But if there is not a compelling basis for value from both the customer's and HBS's points of view, then HBS walks away and devotes its sales efforts to more promising leads.

So it goes throughout the process. Step two, defining requirements, has the business purpose of further qualifying the opportunity. It leads to a go/no-go decision on alignment, with the desired outcome being a requirements document signed by both the customer and HBS. Without that, HBS walks away.

Step three is about committing resources on both sides of the deal. Its business purpose is for HBS to show its commitment to the customer, and for the customer to show at least potential commitment to HBS. The go/no-go decision is about HBS's position in the customer's eyes: Is there evidence of the customer's positive attitude to HBS? The desired outcome is a letter of intent from the customer or HBS's inclusion on the customer's shortlist of providers. Without that, HBS stops expending sales resources and walks away.

Step four begins the breakaway phase with developing solutions. Its business purpose is to demonstrate HBS's superiority over the competition. The go/no-go decision is about differentiation: Has HBS proven that it has the best offering? The desired outcome is an agreement in principle, or HBS walks away.

By the end of the process, step five, the deal has little chance of falling apart, because commitment on both sides has grown and solidified with each preceding step. The business purpose is finalizing the agreement. The go/no-go decision is clear: Is there a signed contract? And the desired outcome, a sales win, is virtually assured.

## Sales as a Science at Honeywell

| Opportunity Status | First Calls | Requirements Definition | Commitment | Solutions Development | Final Negotiation |
|---|---|---|---|---|---|
| Business Purpose | Discovery with the Customer | Qualify/Disqualify the Opportunity | Provide Evidence of Commitment | Finalize Solution | Finalize Details of Agreement |
| Go/No-Go Decision | Qualification: Is there value on both sides of the deal? | Alignment: Do both customer and HBS agree on requirements? | Positioning: Is HBS the customer's choice or on the customer's short list? | Differentiation: Does HBS have the best offer? | Negotiation: Is there a signed contract? |
| Outcome | Signed Decision Schedule | Validated Requirements Document | HBS Short-Listed | Final Proposal | Decision to Move Forward |

© 2011 The Alexander Group, Inc.®

\* \* \*

Now let's turn to Whirlpool and Sony Electronics to see how they, too, advance both the science of sales and the art of the customer relationship.

# Countering Commoditization at Whirlpool and Sony Electronics

Conventional wisdom says that in an industry subject to commoditization, competition on price inevitably erodes customer loyalty to the vanishing point. At first glance, the consumer appliance and electronics industries seem to offer no exceptions to this rule. Yet Whirlpool and Sony Electronics, respectively, have bucked this trend to a remarkable degree.

Perhaps most intriguing, they have done so by independently converging on the same difference maker. In each case, a more productive and scientific sales process has dramatically enhanced their customer relationships and preserved their status as premium brands and market leaders.

\* \* \*

The consumer appliance and consumer electronics industries share many similarities. First, companies in both industries each have two sets of customers. One set comprises end-consumers, reached before a sale primarily through advertising and promotional messages. The other set comprises many different kinds of retailers, including national mass merchants like Sears and Walmart; big-box chains like Lowe's, the Home Depot, and Best Buy; regional chains; and independent dealers all reached through a direct sales force, telesales, and the Internet.

Both industries also feature functional and at least superficial design equivalence among different companies' offerings. Substantive differences in design and user experience may be subtle and not immediately apparent to the consumer. Even in the best case, product innovations are soon reproduced by copycat manufacturers.

Ken Stevens, Sony Electronics senior vice president, observed, "It becomes harder every year for Sony products to be as distinctive as they once were on the shelf. All the digital cameras on the display posts or the flat screen televisions on the wall kind of look the same. They have all copied whatever the most fashionable aesthetics are. You really have to dig into it" to discover the differences. These differences — truly self-guiding menus for setup and operation, "how well products interface with each other" or with a home Wi-Fi network, the speed with which a DVD player recognizes "whether a soundtrack is 5.1 or 7.1 Dolby surround-sound encoded," and so on — are critical to the quality of the user's experience but may not be obvious at first glance. The result is that it is "much more difficult to share the value proposition that makes Sony unique."

Much the same dynamic is at work in the appliance industry. As Whirlpool's Sam Abdelnour shared with us, consumers have usually seen few if any differences in the sea of "white goods" — until recently virtually all appliances were clad in white painted steel and porcelain — from different manufacturers. "Buying an appliance is like shopping for a shovel," one woman in a Whirlpool focus group said. "They all look alike, they all cost about the same, and I can dig a hole with any one of them."

Retailers are not passive conduits to end-consumers. They strive to "create footsteps," in Sam Abdelnour's words, through advertising promotions in cooperation with manufacturers. They also act as gatekeepers, determining what appliance or electronics products consumers see on the sales floor. Finally, retail salespeople, not manufacturers' direct sales forces, are those who interact with consumers on the sales floor. Although consumers may have a brand preference when they enter the store, retailers can often switch them "in the last three feet," as the retail saying goes, to suit their own agendas. Well aware of this reality, consumer appliance and electronics manufacturers regularly offer spiffs (sales performance incentive fees) to encourage retailers and their salespeople to move their products rather than those of competitors.

To overcome these obstacles, both Sony Electronics and Whirlpool look to their sales organizations. Sony's Ken Stevens said:

> A great brand and great products are not enough. We're fortunate to have both, but by themselves they don't take you everywhere you need to go. We're kind of on a bell curve. There's 10 percent of the products that sell by themselves, because they're just so good. There's 10 percent that don't sell at all by themselves; you have to sell them with a bag full of money. Where we spend our time is on the 80 percent of the products in the middle, where they are virtually tied with competition and we have to break the ties.

> An effective selling organization breaks the ties, and the selling organization has to craft what's different, not in a product-centric sense, but in the value-add around the product. What the brand brings to the table, what our service is worth, what our strategic plan is that tells the retailers to invest with us because in the future

*we're going to take them where the competition can't. The value-add that's created is created by the selling organization, not by the product itself.*

For his part, Sam Abdelnour told us, "Because everybody builds pretty good product, we have to find other ways to advantage ourselves." Like Ken Stevens, Abdelnour counts on his sales organization "to deliver all ties. And if we get the ties, we're going to be better off."

To win the ties in the face of encroaching commoditization, Whirlpool and Sony Electronics set their organizations to work on two fronts. Each knew it had to have a deep understanding of, and supply superior solutions to, end-consumer needs and wants, with the goal of making the user experience itself a brand attribute. Each also knew it had to innovate a new way of doing business with retail trade partners.

* * *

Whirlpool developed its understanding of consumers largely through focus groups led by the marketing organization in partnership with sales. Eager to act against the threat of commoditization, the company at first tried to become a "Dominant Consumer Franchise" by adding product features that consumers rated as desirable. But simply tacking on extra features produced a spike in service and repair problems that briefly marred Whirlpool's enviable record of operational excellence. It also offered no sustainable advantage in an appliance industry filled with "fast followers" who could quickly tack the same features onto their machines.

An even more serious issue, Sam Abdelnour recalled, "was that we thought we were going to go around the retail trade and drive consumers into the retailer. We told the trade, 'We're going to give compelling reasons to consumers to come into your stores and buy our products. You're going to have to sell our stuff to them, because we're going to do such a good job that consumers are either going to buy our products from you or they're going to buy them someplace else.'"

Fortunately, Whirlpool's relationship with retailers was strong enough that one of them soon frankly reminded Abdelnour, "This only works if retailers want it to work. If I'm not comfortable with what you're doing, my salespeople will move the consumer to other brands."

At that point, Sam Abdelnour explained:

> *We slowed our process down and started to drive a clearer customer focus around here. We went through a period of time where it was almost a joke. A senior executive would ask somebody in the sales force, "Have you spoken to a customer today?"*
>
> *The answer would be, "I spoke to so-and-so," a retailer.*
>
> *The senior executive would say, "No, I mean an end user."*
>
> *It was an effort to get salespeople to think differently about who the customer was, and recognize that the customer was both the trade and the end user.*

Together with the company's R&D efforts, learning from ongoing focus groups pointed the way to reconceiving product categories and individual products in terms of consumer lifestyle needs and wants, rather than product features. In effect, these investigations were a means of identifying a larger mission that would enable Whirlpool to keep step with consumers as they and society changed. It resulted in three broad but flexible product categories: Fabric care (washers, dryers, irons), food preservation (refrigerators), and food preparation (ovens and countertop appliances).

Through several waves of industry globalization and consolidation, Whirlpool acquired a number of brands from the mid-1980s to the early 2000s, from KitchenAid to Maytag to Jenn-Air. In tandem with its new product categories, Whirlpool aligned its expanded brand portfolio with well-defined consumer segments, positioning the flagship Whirlpool brand for "Active Balancers," KitchenAid for "Home Enthusiasts," and so on. Finally, with new product launches like the front-loading Duet washer and dryer, it succeeded in creating appliances that consumers no longer saw as merely utilitarian and to which they had an emotional connection. For example, one focus group participant referred to her Duet washer as "my little mechanical buddy."

For the Whirlpool sales organization, one key step remained: Taking this enhanced understanding of end-consumers into interactions with its trade retail customers. Sony similarly had to go through a two-stage process of enhancing the consumer-understanding component of its intellectual capital and then carrying that into interactions with retailers.

In chapter 6, "Live the Mission," we discuss how Sony Electronics sees its larger mission, not as electronics, but as entertainment. State-of-the-art consumer electronics technology is simply a means to that end. "We've moved past hardware, we're moving through hardware and software. We've made the jump to entertainment," Ken Stevens told us, adding that "consumers consider us an entertainment company and they trust us with their downtime. There are few more precious commodities for consumers than their off time. If we do anything that jeopardizes that, it's an enormous responsibility on our side."

Stevens neatly caught the transition that consumers are making in a world of broadband connectivity and networked products. In the 1980s and early 1990s, he observed, Sony could still implicitly say to consumers, "What do you want to buy? We can sell it to you." Now the message has become, "What do you want to do? We can help you do it."

Backing up this message requires consultative selling with retailers about how to better manage the consumer experience on the sales floor. It also requires "demystifying" products for consumers, an activity the Sony sales organization participates in directly through the company's Sony Style retail stores and sonystyle.com website. The sales organization then brings the consumer knowledge it gains from Sony Style full circle in its dialogue with electronics retailers. Stevens elaborated:

> Instead of just stuff in boxes, it's stuff that works right out of the box and instant connectivity. Consumers don't recognize Blu-ray [DVD format] from any other ray. Half of them still think it's a fish, I'm sure. But they can tell you they want to watch movies in high definition. They can tell you what they want to do. So it's making sure the top releases are in Blu-ray. It's making sure the Blu-ray DVD player connects easily to a high-definition television set. It's making sure one remote operates the components.
>
> Consumers are very empowered in this equation. You see it on the Internet with 170,000 blogs created every day. They very much want to tell you what's going on now, where they never did before. They have a view to the future they never had before.

According to Sony's research, 85 percent of consumers research electronics products online before they buy. Not all of the information they find online is reliable, however. "So many times consumers get lost" in this process, Ken Stevens said, "and they miss the opportunity to enjoy all of what today's electronics products offer. We are trying to demystify that and make complex technology more transparent.

Sony strives to ensure that its own website answers consumers' needs before and after the purchase. "Not only do we have all the information to support the buying decision," Ken Stevens said, "but after you buy you can go to Sony 101 and learn how to get the best experience out of what you've bought, because we have to win late, too, not just win early. The ultimate goal is to make the consumer experience a brand attribute. So that it's not just that you trust Sony, but that your interaction with Sony makes you want to come back to Sony."

Stevens emphasized the role that Sony's own direct-to-the-consumer selling plays in its efforts with retailers and consumers. "That's why we have sonystyle.com, our online store, and 41 Sony Style stores in the top 40 U.S. markets."

The stores and website function as Sony Electronics' "consumer entertainment labs," venues for both listening to customers about their needs and wants and informing them about the company's entertainment solutions. "They're our message directly to the consumer," Stevens said, "and the consumer's message directly to us. Sony Style has three tenets: Brand, educate, and revenue. And revenue's the third."

In this regard Sony is happy to interact with a customer in its Sony Style stores, only to see the customer leave in search of a better price at Best Buy or another retailer. "If a consumer says, 'I'm going to go to Best Buy because it's cheaper,' we say, 'They're a great retailer.' The consumer is better educated in our value equation, and that's fine. It's only not good if they go to Best Buy and buy somebody else's stuff."

In fact, Sony wants to improve at facilitating hand-offs to Best Buy and other retailers. Stevens said, "Our work going forward is figuring out how to hold the consumer's hand a little bit longer and say, 'Where is your local Best Buy? Oh, look, they have it in stock and we've reserved it for you. You can go pick it up.' That's the next piece of where we have to take that."

As this comment indicates, the potential for enhanced consumer loyalty that Whirlpool and Sony saw would be frittered away if the two companies could not also use their increasingly sophisticated understanding of end-consumers to enhance the loyalty of their respective retail trade partners. Whirlpool's Sam Abdelnour said, "As we learned more about how consumers were changing and how we had to change to earn and increase their loyalty to our brands, we realized that if we could help our trade partners with the same transformation, we could change our role from an appliance manufacturer to that of a trusted business partner."

Speaking to the potential benefits of leveraging the sales organization's supply chain expertise together with its consumer understanding, Whirlpool's David Provost added, "We wanted to get on the same side of the table with the trade and look at the customer equation on their sales floors, and then bring our intellectual capital to the relationship and help them improve their business. That way we could improve business for both of us and enhance customer loyalty to both our brands."

Sony Electronics recognized the same imperative as part of its mission to respect and enhance consumers' downtime. "We have to show everybody, retailers and consumers, how to turn that downtime into uptime," Ken Stevens said. "That's our job as the industry leader in our part of the entertainment business."

The desire to be their retailers' trusted business partners and to be recognized by them as industry leaders had long set Whirlpool and Sony Electronics apart from their respective competitors. Despite its brief stumble with retailers over the "Dominant Consumer Franchise" program described above, Whirlpool "has always had a relationship with the trade where there was a genuine sense that we were the white hats," Whirlpool's David Provost told us. "We were the first ones in the appliance industry to talk about 'trade partners.'"

Likewise, Sony's Ken Stevens observed that because of its brand stature and breadth of offerings, "Sony often represents 50 percent or more of a retailer's business in consumer electronics." Sony accordingly set a long-term strategy focused "on the overall prosperity of the retail accounts, driving our revenue growth through the accounts' success and their growth," and took pains to communicate that to the accounts.

Whirlpool and Sony Electronics thus had a foundation of trust with the retail trade in their industries. They would need every bit of that trust to get retailers' buy-in on a radical new sales model.

## *From Sell-In to Sell-Through*

As we've been emphasizing, making sales more of a science is about making it a more fact-based, reliable, predictable — and thus more profitable — process. The changes that Sony and Whirlpool made to their sales models exemplify this approach.

When Sam Abdelnour joined Whirlpool in the late 1970s, fresh out of college, "The idea was a loaded dealer is a loyal dealer. Fill the dealer's warehouse up, and he's got no choice but to sell your products. You might sell somebody five months' worth of inventory, and then not do business with them except for fill-in type activity."

Unfortunately, Abdelnour continued, "That's tough on manufacturing. That's tough on finance. It's tough on everybody. It impacts cash flow." It is also tough on the trade customer: Unsold inventories in both the appliance dealer's and the manufacturer's warehouses represent frozen assets that cannot earn a return. The downsides of this sales model emerged more and more clearly from the mid-1980s onwards, as global commoditization and discount pricing pressured the consumer appliance industry.

The consumer electronics industry, which also operated on a "fill the dealer's warehouse" sales model, went through much the same upheaval in the 1990s, with the additional pressure of a transition from analog to digital products. The digital revolution made it even easier for copycat manufacturers to replicate premium brand offerings and undercut their pricing.

Independently, Whirlpool and Sony Electronics each recognized that a viable sales model would be, in Sam Abdelnour's words, "less about sell-in and more about creating sell-through at the point of sale so it replenishes itself." The way to secure loyalty from trade customers was not to load their warehouses, but to "help them measure their business better, help them plan and forecast better." In short, the leaner and more profitable the trade customer's inventory became, the leaner and more profitable Whirlpool could become.

Likewise at Sony, Ken Stevens and his colleagues saw the potential for what they called "demand-based selling:"

> *We had to figure out another way for retailers and us to make money, and we thought the best way was through the supply chain process. How could we help retailers take inventory out? How could*

*we show them the balance sheet side of savings, in order to show our value as opposed to somebody else's?*

Describing the discussions within Sony's sales organization, Ken Stevens added that a sales consultant, the Alexander Group's Mike Miller (disclosure: Co-author Gary Tubridy is a principal of AGI), helped crystallize Sony's new challenge and opportunity: "Mike Miller sat in a meeting with us and said, 'From what you are describing, the sales job is becoming more one of asset management.' And it was like the phrase that pays. Asset management became a core operating principle of the sales organization."

At both Whirlpool and Sony it was the sales organization that led the change from a sell-in to a sell-through approach. Sony's marketing organization was resistant, Ken Stevens recalled:

*Marketing was focused on getting the stuff out of our warehouse and into the dealer's warehouse. From the selling side we said, "Look, we can't create a motion for that stuff to leave the dealer's warehouse. We can't fill that warehouse again, because it's just going to be full."*

*And our pitch back to marketing was that we wanted to start saying to our customers, "Don't buy a thousand, and we'll give you two points of advertising funds and one more point of margin. Let's create a demand plan for a hundred, and we know you'll buy a thousand because you'll sell them."*

*That took some good, solid internal selling to our counterparts in marketing.*

At a company without a true customer focus, that might have been the end of it. But at Sony, in Stevens's words, "The marketing folks said, 'Okay, we're watching every minute, but if you really think that's the right way to go, we'll go with you.'"

\* \* \*

To share supply chain expertise with trade customers, the Whirlpool and Sony Electronics sales organizations first had to acquire it. The Whirlpool sales organization was able to do so internally, thanks to the company's acquisition-driven alignment of procurement, manufacturing, and design resources across global manufacturing platforms and a vastly expanded brand portfolio.

The Sony Electronics sales organization had to look outside, however. Ken Stevens told us, "We knew we had to move in a different direction and focus on supply chain. [Having made that decision], the first thing we did is acknowledge that we didn't know the first thing about supply chain. We could barely spell supply chain."

To close the gap, Sony looked for the best available expertise and "discovered that the University of Tennessee had the premier supply chain program in the United States and that John Meltzer, a professor at its business school, was the guru of supply chain."

Initial consultation with Professor Meltzer led to sending all the sales reps to the University of Tennessee for six courses in supply chain management, "from the basics of forecasting to the difference between a supply chain process with adaptive smoothing and without adaptive smoothing." Moreover, Sony invited trade customers to take advantage of an abbreviated version of the same resources. Gradually Sony developed its supply-chain expertise to the point where it could move the training in-house.

Last but not least, Whirlpool and Sony had to persuade trade customers to embrace a new sales model.

\* \* \*

To start the effort of engaging trade customers about the consumer purchasing experience and other aspects of their business, Sam Abdelnour led a group, including David Provost, in an all-day meeting with one of Whirlpool's large regional trade partners. The Whirlpool group began its presentation by "showing the trade partner what his average sales volumes (ASVs) and average selling prices (ASPs) were compared to his competitors. We showed him what his inventory levels and his turns of inventory were compared to theirs."

Sam Abdelnour continued:

> *The trade partner actually got out of his seat and walked up to the screen the information was projected onto. He looked at it for what seemed like an eternity without saying anything. Eventually he asked, "Where did you get this much information about my business?"*

*I said, "From you. You and your competitors all send us your point of sale information every day. And we can take that information and combine it with internal and external resources, and package it into something useful for you."*

Sam Abdelnour told the trade partner that Whirlpool intended to share the same non-proprietary information with his competitors, if they were interested in seeing it. As Abdelnour explained to us, "We want to help the whole trade to improve, not select partners here and there."

With consumer-focus-group film and other materials, Abdelnour's group then explained what Whirlpool had learned "not only about what Mrs. Jones wants in appliances, how desirable certain features are to her, how important design and style and color are to her, but also about what she thinks of the experience of shopping for appliances." As Abdelnour elaborated, he told the trade partner:

*Let us show you what Mrs. Jones thinks of your sales environment.*

*She hates the fact that your parking lots are not lit. She's discouraged when she sees your salespeople standing in the doorway smoking, because she's fearful about crossing that line. She doesn't like being trapped in the corner of your store where the refrigerators are all lined up, because she doesn't feel she has an escape route.*

Abdelnour's fear that day was that the trade partner "was just going to throw up over all this." Instead, "It blew him and his associates away. In fact, it blew them away to the point where they now wanted us to collaborate with them on store design and on store display, and on finding ways to attract consumers and keep them in their stores longer."

Scaling up the effort to engage trade customers in improving their businesses, Sam Abdelnour "went out on the lecture circuit [and] talked to thousands of trade partners about the competency Whirlpool was developing around the consumer and the purchasing experience." Now that Whirlpool was proposing to work with trade partners on consumer issues, rather than go around them, the response was entirely different. Abdelnour knew an important milestone had been reached, when he addressed the Nationwide Appliance Buying Group on an unseasonably hot February day in Orlando, FL:

*It felt like 155 degrees that day. The humidity was 112. I'm about to address 1,200 people, and I'm wondering if they're going to accept what I have to say as a rational thought for how to run their businesses better. I was expressing my misgivings to David Provost, who was handling the slides for me, and he encouraged me to "go out there and do it."*

*But that was the beginning of something different that separated us from our competitors. Because we got over four hundred inquiries from people at that meeting wanting individual assessments of their businesses, wanting to understand the consumer better, wanting to know if we had richer, more specific data to present to them.*

Not all trade customers responded to such communications with immediate enthusiasm. David Provost recalled how when he talked to one retailer about how consumers disliked the appliance shopping experience and the confusing selections they were offered, he heard back, "So, David, what's wrong with that? We confuse them on the sales floor, they ask for help, and we sell them what we have in inventory and what we make the most money on. Life is good."

Provost concluded, "I thanked him for his candor. But I said, 'Consumers are changing, and you're leaving an opportunity on the table. If you don't figure that out, one of your competitors will.'"

Overall, in Sam Abdelnour's words, "There was a level of belief and trust in us on the part of the trade, if not always immediately to the degree that we hoped for," that allowed Whirlpool to continue the conversation with retailers. In fact, retailers tended to respond in a sequence of stages, as Abdelnour explained:

*The same thing almost always happens when we go through this process with a customer. After the first meeting, there's shock. That shock is lessened by the second meeting, because they know what kind of information we have. By the third time we meet, they want more. They offer to give us even more detailed data, so we can give them better insight into the way their business is performing.*

The engagement with trade customers grew even stronger, Abdelnour said, when Whirlpool "began doing focus groups about individual trade partners' businesses. We had the principals behind the glass watching, so no longer was it data on a slide. It was consumers talking about their very own business."

Reconfiguring an appliance sales floor to display products as they might look in consumers' homes is expensive. Fewer products can be shown, because each display takes up more space. "But if you can convert that space into higher average sale prices," Abdelnour noted, "a better mix of products that delivers more bottom-line dollars, isn't it worth the investment?" Only through disciplined application of the science of sales could Whirlpool demonstrate to retailers how worthwhile an investment this would be.

\* \* \*

At Sony Electronics, too, not all retail partners saw the benefits of the sell-through model. Some were too wedded to their familiar way of doing business, and for the most part they have not survived, Ken Stevens said, "because they didn't see the trend," despite Sony's efforts to "educate them and say, 'This is where we all need to move.'"

But thanks to the trust Sony had with retailers in general, the vast majority of accounts, including "Best Buy, Sears/Kmart, Target, and Walmart," as well as a host of other retailers from independent dealers to regional chains, "recognized the same things we did, so we could build partnerships with them to achieve tremendous success. We showed the retailers a different way to make money at a time when consumer electronics products were not holding their value long enough for them to be sure to make it."

Note that in redefining their relationships with retailers around sophisticated asset management, Whirlpool and Sony focused their efforts on the most important strategic accounts. They put dedicated teams against big national retailers and large regional chains, where they could maximize their influence on the retail industry, obtain leverage with the largest number of consumers, and achieve the biggest impact on their own bottom lines. With allowances for the differences in industry, it's an approach to key account management that bears comparison with the astute allocation of sales resources, as noted above, practiced by Cisco, FedEx, HBS, HP, Oracle, and Xerox. Advancing the science of sales is not something that happens only in high-tech industries, by any means.

# Internal Sales Asset Management

Sony and Whirlpool transformed the way their trade partners managed inventory. For the two sales organizations, this was an innovative form of external asset management. To exploit the advantages of this sales model, they also had to manage their internal assets in creative ways. More generally, putting the right resources into the right sales channels is one of many characteristics that Sony and Whirlpool share with other high-performing sales organizations. It is a central aspect of advancing the science of sales in order to support and advance the art of the customer relationship.

\* \* \*

For Sony's largest customers, Ken Stevens told us, there is key account management with "dedicated supply-chain groups working specifically with Best Buy, Sears/Kmart, Target, and Walmart." For regional retail chains "there are centralized resources, but not dedicated resources." And there is a roving "field training organization of 60 people," who work with various retailers to "make sure displays are right and help train the retailer's salespeople."

In addition, Ken Stevens told us, there is "what we used to refer to as telesales and now call our Integrated Sales Network." This group handles not only "small independent retailers" but also some accounts "that may do multimillion dollar volume buying only five or six models from us and don't need the traditional type of sales call."

Speaking to the need to "manage these different channels in harmony with each other," Stevens emphasized that "it is important to recognize how accounts are interdependent on each other" for Sony, given its extensive product line across a wide range of price points. As an example, he mentioned how a groundbreaking product like Sony's organic light-emitting diode (OLED) television will first largely be sold only through specialty audio-visual and high-end home theater dealers before it eventually migrates into mass market outlets. The mix of products available through different retail channels "helps make Sony the viable and desirable brand that is so successful in a Best Buy store."

Making the supply chain a virtuous cycle from Sony to its retail customers also required a significant change in sales force compensation. Ron Boire, Sony's president of consumer electronics sales when it decided to implement the sell-through model, told us, "Sony moved to a process in which 50 percent of salespeople's compensation is based on retail customer scorecards with metrics like on-time delivery, in stock, gross margin return on inventory [the key retail performance metric], and sales forecast accuracy."

Sony's adjustment of its sales compensation metrics provides a superb example of combining the science of sales with the art of the customer relationship. It shows how positive the results can be when you not only identify the behavior necessary to deliver value but also complement that with a program and tools to support the behavior. For Sony to realize the potential of its lean-inventory sell-through approach, its salespeople had to reshape their relationships with retail customers. The new compensation scheme was an essential means for advancing this process. As Boire summed up, "When you change the basis of people's paychecks, it really is remarkable how fast they change their behavior."

\* \* \*

To exploit its new sell-through model fully, Whirlpool also needed to realign sales resources against trade customer segments. Accordingly, Sam Abdelnour said, "One of the things that we organized around is key account management."

This realignment required shifting resources that had been devoted to small accounts to big national and regional accounts. Whirlpool still had sellers call on small accounts face-to-face, because "people like to buy from people," in David Provost's words. But it could "skinny up" on those calls and earn greater trade customer satisfaction with Internet and telesales support. David Provost elaborated:

> The small accounts had Whirlpool sellers calling on them. But they could never get their salespeople on the phone, because they were calling on larger customers. The small accounts would have to leave messages with their questions and requests. The salespeople didn't have the answers at their fingertips, they had to research them, and that meant Whirlpool people leaving messages for each other. And then finally the salespeople had to get back to the accounts. It was very unproductive.

*Since we delivered Internet and telesales solutions to the small accounts, they get their answers on the first call or the first log-on, because the telesales folks have the answers right there on their screens or the customers have it right there on the web site. The small accounts can get the status of their orders, pricing, or whatever they need. Now there is a very productive situation for them and us.*

## *Conclusion*

Hewlett-Packard, Whirlpool, Sony Electronics, Honeywell Building Solutions, Cisco, FedEx, Oracle, Xerox—in chapters 3 and 4 we have seen how these sales organizations renewed and enhanced their customer relationships with a rigorous sales process. From a bird's-eye perspective it is clear that sales roles have become more complex and demanding across the B2B and B2C landscape. Up close, the distinction that emerges between the winning sales organizations and the also-rans is how committed the former are to engineering sales processes and fulfilling sales roles in a customer-motivated way.

* * *

Perhaps you have noticed the absence in this and the preceding chapter of any discussion of experimentation, the fundamental activity of science. We have been silent on this issue, not because great sales organizations fail to experiment as they advance the science of sales and the art of the customer relationship, but because they experiment so much and so often that it deserves a chapter of its own. Let's now look closely at how sales experimentation contributes to sales excellence.

## HOW GREAT SALES ORGANIZATIONS ADVANCE THE SCIENCE OF SALES AND THE ART OF THE CUSTOMER RELATIONSHIP

- Fact-based decision making that keeps the human element in mind and never loses sight of customer needs.

- Focused, flexible resource allocation across customer segments and sales channels.

- Matching sales models, including the mix of channels and of generalist and specialist sales roles, to evolving customer needs.

- Leveraging increasingly sophisticated intellectual capital in roles where an old-style generalist seller's responsibility would have been largely confined to relationship management.

- Continuous improvement of sales analytics, sales processes, and sales operations.

- Alignment of individual and organizational performance measures.

# CHAPTER 5
# Make Loud Mistakes

**FAILURE PAVES THE WAY TO SUCCESS.** Great sales organizations therefore encourage repeated failures on the part of sales reps, sales managers, and senior sales executives.

We don't mean that they encourage, or allow, their people to repeat the same mistakes over and over again. But great sales organizations understand that the only way to identify, create, and deliver superior customer value in an environment of continual change is through continual experimentation. They not only accept, but even celebrate, the mistakes that are a necessary part of this learning process. As we noted at the end of the previous chapter, experimentation, the hallmark of the scientific method, also characterizes elite sales organizations' efforts to advance the science of sales and the art of the customer relationship.

In this regard consistently high-performing sales organizations:

- Always try to look around the corner to anticipate changes in customer needs and market conditions, and are always willing to change sales models and sales processes accordingly.

- Refine and discover best practices through frequent pilot projects using a fail-or-scale model.

- Create a nimble, cost-effective learning organization with a focus on "making loud mistakes" and "failing quickly," as two senior sales leaders respectively put it.

- Hire people who are temperamentally suited to creative trial-and-error experimentation.

- Empower the sales force to succeed through failure by celebrating and rewarding learning from honest mistakes.

- Understand that the only unacceptable mistakes are those that are repeated.

\* \* \*

Addressing these imperatives, and sharing the memorable turn of phrase we've taken for our chapter title, Genzyme's Dan Regan said:

*I always try to keep in mind something that I learned from my first grade teacher, Mrs. Kashegian. She told us, "Make loud mistakes." Your culture has to empower people to do that. If you hire the right people and you're very clear what the mission is, and you empower them to make a lot of mistakes in an environment that allows them to admit them and learn from them, you're going to go far.*

The unpredictable, uncontrollable nature of the business environment makes it essential to hire and develop creative, resilient people who revel in experimentation. As Oracle's Keith Block observed, "You're never done. There's always something you can improve." A sales model that worked in the past may need adjustment to remain viable, or new market circumstances may render it obsolete and require an entirely new one. Constant inspection and experimentation are the only ways to determine what needs to be done. Block said:

*We always ask, "Can we do better? What did we learn? What works? What doesn't work? What do we need to adjust?"*

*Whenever we have planning sessions, I challenge the team to throw out the conventional wisdom. Every year we try to change something, just so people don't get stale. So we experiment.*

In addition to planned experimentation, a sales organization and its people must also be willing to experiment in response to suddenly emerging crises, big or small. High-performing sales organizations accept this imperative and take it as an opportunity to separate the wheat from the chaff in terms of their personnel. Speaking in terms we heard echoed by many of the senior sales executives we interviewed, MasterCard's Gary Flood said:

*One of the biggest tests that I use is when something really goes wrong, can you work it out with the customer? Challenging situations are bound to happen. We don't put people in the penalty box for that; we want them to navigate through it. Even if it's very challenging, you can work through it if you listen to the voice of the customer. We tell our people, "Put everything aside other than what's important to the customer." That's their job.*

As we already saw in chapter 2, "Speak Clearly — and Carry a Big Carrot," SAP Business Objects' Gary Lorden seeks to hire people with "a blue-collar mentality" precisely because of their willingness to take the initiative and experiment to solve problems. This is the sort of sales person who responds to failure by saying, "It's … up to me, I've got to figure out something." It doesn't matter how many failures a sales person has, he added, "[a]s long as you're growing and learning. If you're making the same mistakes over and over again, that's a different story."

Once a sales organization has such people, it must make sure the culture encourages and supports their experimentation. Salespeople must feel free not only to admit mistakes but to also speak up about problems they see anywhere in the sales organization or the wider company, from HR practices to the customer relationship and sales model to the viability of product and service sets.

Acknowledging that experimentation may take an organization into "gray areas, and yes, that is uncomfortable," Genzyme's Dan Regan remarked, "If you have a culture that's so tight that people, when they do make a mistake, can't let anybody know, you never learn from them." As we discussed in chapter 2, when a survey showed that Genzyme sales reps felt that the organization made it difficult to speak freely, Regan and his colleagues responded by establishing a sales and marketing advisory committee staffed by sales reps and others on a rotating basis, and took pains, explicitly and implicitly, to show that it was indeed safe for sales reps to voice their concerns. As Genzyme's Joe Brennan noted, a sales organization cannot thrive for long if it doesn't "listen to the field" about what is working well and what is not.

All of the executives we spoke to for this book agreed that a great sales organization has to have a culture of risk-taking. Dan Regan said, "If your business is worth investing in, it is worth taking some risks in." Risk-taking means that "you have to be willing to go out there with five crazy ideas and fall on your face with three or four of them." Accordingly, Regan said:

*I am a believer in celebrating failure. I am a believer in holding somebody up when they fall on their face and saying, "This guy tried this. He fell on his face. It did not work. Everybody give him a round of applause."*

*It shocks the hell out of people when you do something like that. They say, "What is he talking about?" And I am saying it is okay to make a mistake, because — let me tell you, the next week that rep did not fall on his face — he ended up jumping over three hurdles and he got the account. Boom! That is a beautiful thing.*

Similarly, the most striking thing we heard from Ken Stevens of Sony Electronics was his insisting, "You have to empower people to fail. People can't be afraid. If they're afraid, they won't fail. If they don't fail, they only get to about 80 percent of where they could go."

The implicit message is clear: If its people are afraid to fail, if they don't regularly fail in the course of creative experimentation, a sales organization only gets to about 80 percent of where it could go. It's not just a matter of working atmosphere and attitude. To support productive risk-taking, sales leaders must limit the impact of organizational bureaucracy and zealously seek to enhance and enlarge sales reps' selling time (for more on these issues, see chapter 2).

Ken Stevens remarked to us that giving sales reps the freedom to fail is part of linking empowerment and accountability. As with his views on leading from the front (see chapter 1, "Lead from the Front"), Oracle's Keith Block stressed that sales leadership's acceptance of accountability, "act[ing] like it's your own business," drives a culture of effective experimentation. Reiterating that "good leadership behavior cascades down" through an organization, he pointed first of all to Oracle's founder and CEO, Larry Ellison, for his fostering of innovation and his ensuring that bureaucracy does not throttle necessary trial and error:

> *We're a $23 billion company, and we act like a $50 million startup. If I want to make an investment, I just go to Larry and explain why I think it's a good idea. If it doesn't work, we'll adjust it or kill it. But Larry's not afraid to try things. That's one of the great things about this place.*

Brookstone's Ron Boire and SAP Business Objects' Greg Lorden, among other executives, spoke of the positive effect that empowering people to fail has on their morale, effort, and effectiveness. In Lorden's words, "What is working with the salespeople is that we love experiments. I tell them, 'You've got a good idea for what you need in your territory, okay, go do it.'" The willingness to support a creative risk and not punish a failure, he added, "proves that we're open, that it's not 'my way or the highway,' that we'll change." This perspective in turn boosts acceptance of organization-wide experiments and changes, Lorden said, adding: "We made some positive changes to the comp plan, and I'm getting a lot more miles out of it than it's costing."

Openness to taking risks and transparency about the results enable a sales organization to minimize the costs of failed experiments and maximize benefits from successes. In the first regard, this is what Genzyme's Dan Regan had in mind in referring to "loud mistakes." If something is not working, Regan added, "raise your hand early. Be transparent, then come out and try to get it right next time."

A number of sales executives we spoke to distinguished between learning from smart mistakes and perpetuating dumb ones. Ambiguity in the market may make it difficult to decide which is which, and transparency is the only way to walk the "fine line" between pulling the plug on an effort too early and waiting too long to do so.

Making the same point, Sony Electronics' Ken Stevens used the phrase "fail quickly." He explained:

> You have to tell the sales reps, "Fail quickly." Not every idea is going to work. If you're going to fail, fail quickly. Don't hang on because it's your favorite idea. If the idea is failing, see it, cut it, move in another direction. If you fail over a long term, you cost a lot of money. You can fail quickly, and it's not a big hit to the company, it's not a tragedy to you personally. It doesn't send a terrible message about your ability to run a business. That's okay. But if you hang on to an idea that's not working, it is a reflection of your ability to recognize the business opportunity.

The payoff for creative risk-taking is the discovery and development of new best practices, following the experimental model of "fail or scale." At Genzyme, for example, Joe Brennan shared the story of how an experiment with one rep led to larger changes. Needing to gain traction for its products in the field of gynecological oncology, Genzyme wanted to reach influential specialists at New York hospitals, where the sales reps were comparatively inexperienced. Brennan explained:

> We did a pilot with a Philadelphia rep who was extremely clinically competent. We gave him six accounts in New York to work with the local sales reps, and we paid double commission for a year.

*The Philadelphia rep still had to maintain his own territory. He took the train up to New York, and he didn't hit all six accounts, but he hit most of them. The average rep grows a whole territory $250,000 a year. We expected zero growth, and he grew those few accounts $450,000.*

*So it was overwhelmingly successful. Plus, we could see the positive effect on the whole gynecological-oncology community from reaching these influential doctors.*

*The Philadelphia rep became national key account director with six people working with him, just calling on the key opinion leaders in gynecological-oncology. The result was we got much more traction at important hospitals and medical centers all across the country."*

Similarly, at SAP Business Objects, Greg Lorden told us that a regional sales manager "experimented with what he called the mid-quarter funnel." Instead of looking at the 10 or so prospective deals that might be identified at the beginning of a quarter, this approach provided "a snapshot on a more focused area of what could actually solidify." Scaled up, this became a new best practice across the entire sales organization.

Best practices can emerge from failed experiments, as results indicate the potential for adjusting a sales model or redirecting an initiative. In "fail or scale" mode, it also frequently happens that a successful experiment triggers fresh experiments in new areas. For example, let's revisit Oracle's shift from generalist to specialist sales roles, which we explored earlier. Experiments with specialized roles opened up the possibility for "specializing even further," Keith Block told us, with "progressively more granularity in our sales force" in new product and service areas, such as software security. At the time of our initial conversation, Block was shaping up a "security solutions sales force" to meet the increasing customer need in that area. Yet another form of sales specialization Oracle is considering is the creation of "industry business units to project and leverage firepower" where deep expertise is a differential advantage. One good idea leads to another.

On the other hand, as we also saw, the shift to specialist sales roles did not prevent Oracle from nimbly retrieving and refashioning the best of its old generalist model when appropriate. To coordinate multiple sales specialists and prevent "consternation" on the part of some large customers with centralized buying, Oracle "picked the [sales specialist] with the best relationship with the customer and said, 'We're anointing you the greater amongst equals." The experiment of creating a "key account director" for such accounts worked so well that Oracle scaled it up as a formal program for large, complex accounts with centralized buying.

As this example shows, experimentation must become a regular habit if a sales organization wants to stay ahead of the curve on changing customer needs. Now let's dive down more deeply into a sales organization that has made piloting experiments on a "fail or scale" plan a part of its basic identity.

## "We Are Always Testing": How Pitney Bowes Pilots and Scales Winning Sales Initiatives

Pitney Bowes has been a fixture of the business landscape for so long — it was founded in 1920 and is a charter member of the Standard & Poor's 500 and the Fortune 500 — that it is easy to take it for granted or dismiss it as stodgy and old fashioned. But the company has only survived — and thrived — for so long by continually evolving to keep pace with changing customer needs. In fact, Pitney Bowes is the trendsetter in products, services, and technology in a $250 billion global mailstream industry; innovations in sales have played a major role in keeping the company at the forefront of managing both physical and digital information flows across businesses, from B2B and B2C.

From the turn of the century to our interviews in 2008, Pitney Bowes achieved average revenue growth of seven percent annually, much of it organic growth, and increased total revenues from $3.7 billion in 2000 to $6.3 billion in 2008. In addition, it produced rising free cash flow averaging over $600 million per year and consistent dividend growth, performing well through the ups and downs of the business cycle. In the daunting economic downturn that began with the 2007/2008 crisis in the sub-prime mortgage market, Pitney Bowes managed to hold its own.

Behind the numbers there has been significant change from a rigid command-and-control hierarchy to a sales culture that encourages experimentation, combining a creative willingness to pilot new approaches with a Darwinian rigor in culling out the losers and scaling up the winners. Rob Fruithandler, then senior vice president of sales operations, told us how Pitney Bowes's U.S. sales organization keeps finding new and better ways to deliver value to customers and earn revenues and profits for the company and its shareholders. He emphasized the Pitney Bowes sales organization's flexibility in four areas: Leadership and decision making, training and coaching, segmentation and sales coverage, and learning from both successes and failures.

## *Leadership and Decision Making*

Like executives we spoke to at other high-performing, customer-motivated companies, Fruithandler agreed that successful change and growth must be led and supported by the C-suite. What is especially intriguing in the Pitney Bowes story is how that leadership is shared and distributed throughout the sales organization.

As Fruithandler put it, "The leadership of this company recognized that business as usual was no longer viable. So they embraced change." Several factors in the general business environment and customers' needs contributed to this recognition. The B2B and B2C mailstreams are no longer only physical documents and packages but contain a growing digital component. And much of the B2C physical mailstream has become less transactional, as consumers receive statements and pay bills online, and more promotional. "The importance of that to us is that we see that change happening and we're managing the business to that change."

Managing to the change required that Pitney Bowes acquire new capabilities in software, content production, service management, and consulting, and that it meld them with the company's core mailing business. It also required greater flexibility, creativity, and (no contradiction here) results-based discipline in the sales organization to craft compelling value propositions from the new mix of offerings in order to achieve desired growth. Put all that together, and it meant a much sharper focus on changing customer needs. In Rob Fruithandler's words, "Meeting the growth challenge means continuously peeling back the layers of customers' and prospects' businesses to understand how you can build more value in the solutions that you're offering." Especially in tough economic times, "customers are making more value-based decisions, and we have to reflect that in the services and solutions that we sell."

A crucial part of this effort was evolving away from "a very rigid, centralized type of organization. One of a number of changes in this regard involved recruiting people at every level — field sales reps, local and district sales managers, and senior executives — for one year assignments, in addition to their normal duties, on a compensation advisory board and a marketing advisory team. As we noted in chapter 1, "Lead from the Front," this innovation gives Pitney Bowes's sales reps and sales leaders joint ownership of strategic goals and tactical decisions. It also "breaks down the civil war between different functions, especially between the field sales force and marketing," helping the sales reps to understand the marketing organization's point of view on sales promotions such as very low or even zero percent financing.

The learning goes both ways between sales and marketing, Fruithandler emphasized:

> I've got about 70 people in my marketing organization, and they are all to be out in the field with sales reps and customers at least a couple of days a quarter. That keeps them honest and helps them understand what customers are saying and how sales is using the tools they're providing. Having involvement with the sales force and customers gives marketing a better framework to get things done. You have to connect the dots between customers, sales, and marketing; it's a three-legged stool.

One of the greatest benefits of the advisory teams is that they create sponsors within the sales force for new sales and marketing initiatives. "We now have folks in the field who are advocates to their peers," Fruithandler observed. "So things are embraced a lot easier by the sales reps, as opposed to Moses coming down from the mountain and saying, 'I'm from the home office, and here's your marketing plan, here's your compensation plan.'"

To make sure that the sales organization walks the walk, as well as talks the talk, the leadership team has seen to it that a percentage of senior sales executives' incentive compensation is pegged to supporting the advisory teams.

"Prior to 2001," Fruithandler said, "the desire of the field organization to pilot things and take on change was significantly less than it is today. We now have people in the business who are very interested in doing things differently. They have a vision of what the organization can be; they have the desire to make the hard changes. And to a large degree, the sales organization as a whole has been modified. The perspective has shifted dramatically in the last several years. It's been a huge cultural change."

# *Training and Coaching*

Another common thread in our discussions with the leaders of top sales organizations is that new approaches depend on effective training and coaching to succeed. Just as Pitney Bowes recognized that changes in the mailstream industry required a new mix of products and services, it also recognized that it had to elevate its sales messages and interactions from customers' mail rooms to their C-suites. As Fruithandler explained, sales reps accordingly had to shift from pitching the "feeds and speeds" of mail machines to "talking to the CFO and the CIO" about business applications and solutions.

That was a challenging transition for the sales force to make, and Pitney Bowes sought to do so with "revamped hiring and training — and retraining." In the process, the sales organization also hoped to halt an exodus of sales talent. At a time when the sales force had around 2,500 sales reps, three to four percent were defecting on a monthly basis. Fruithandler said, "We had a scenario where every month 70 to 80 salespeople walked out the door. That number at its height was 100 per month. We had to stop the bleeding."

Exit interviews with departing sales reps revealed two main sources of discontent. The sales reps felt hamstrung in their selling and were not making enough money. And new sales reps especially felt they weren't being given the tools, training, and coaching they needed to succeed.

In what has become a regular practice of using experimental pilots to test new approaches, Pitney Bowes piloted a new training program for "a year and a half," continuously revising it and measuring its results against a control group. "We tracked the results of a group that went through the old training and a group that went through the new training," Fruithandler added, "and it was hands-down clear that the new group of salespeople was better equipped to tell the Pitney Bowes story and better able to sell."

The pilot period was long enough to show that the new training had a significant side benefit: It lowered costly turnover in the sales force. Because sales reps with the new training "were selling more and making more money," Fruithandler explained, "they were more likely to stay. Pitney Bowes has a pay-for-performance model. We don't give you a whole lot of money in base salary, but if you do a good job of selling, the sky's the limit. The new training made sales reps so much more equipped to hit the ground running. Of the initial class of sixteen, we lost a couple from the field sales force because they got promoted fast. It was not because they weren't performing."

The new training program was then made standard for all hires, and also became the template for retraining veteran sales reps.

One of the insights the sales organization took away from its training pilots was the importance of coaching by front-line sales managers (for more on this crucial issue, see chapter 2, "Speak Clearly — and Carry a Big Carrot"). Rob Fruithandler told us, "We're a big believer that front-line manager coaching is the biggest key to success. The effectiveness of sales reps who get three hours of quality coaching time a month from their managers goes up exponentially over sales reps who don't get that coaching."

The sales organization took several steps to improve coaching by front-line managers. It mandated that managers and sales reps have regular sales effectiveness planning meetings, but rather than decree that one size fits all, it varied the frequency of the meetings depending on a sales rep's experience and track record, starting with as often as once a week for new sales reps and their managers.

In major metropolitan markets, Pitney Bowes also established a "training-development-manager pilot," with select front-line sales managers dedicated to ramping up new sales reps for six to nine months, rather than the usual mix of new hires and veterans. Instead of competing for a sales manager's attention with senior sales reps who were closing deals, the new sales reps "are all learning together, they're all assured of getting time, and as the other sales teams need new folks, they become like the Triple-A farm team." The pilot has "been very successful in some markets and not in others." Accordingly, the sales organization will "continue the pilot in places where it's worked," and seek to fine tune it for wider use, because "in today's selling environment you have to be willing to try new and different things."

The sales organization naturally has its eye on sales reps who are good candidates to become sales managers. But an intriguing aspect of the process to develop front-line sales managers is that the selection is not solely made from the top down. Instead, any rep can opt in and self-select for a program that Pitney Bowes calls "Elite Today." To progress through the program, sales reps have to pass an increasingly rigorous set of hurdles, but the opportunity for self-selection at the start helps ensure that talented prospects are not missed.

Fruithandler explained:

> *Every sales rep can raise their hand and join Elite Today. Everybody who raises their hand comes together in a meeting, they get a little training, and then they're assigned some project work to give them a chance to show that they're really interested.*
>
> *Those who actually complete their projects successfully and show us they have some of the behavioral attributes that we like to see in a manager, which are different in terms of empathy and so on from what we're looking for in a sales person, advance to our Top Gun program. Top Gun brings them to our centralized training facility in Atlanta, GA, and that's where they start to get management training and we start to filter out whether they really have or can acquire the skills to be a manager.*
>
> *We continue that process, including both e-learning and in-classroom learning, to develop district-director-level managers with our Edge Program. So it's not the old, "Here's the relocation package; now you're a district director; go get 'em."*

The Pitney Bowes sales organization tracks the effectiveness of its sales rep and sales manager training with sales-time measures. Characteristically for Pitney Bowes, the sales-time measures were piloted first and then scaled up after they proved their worth.

## *A Place to Go and a Story to Tell: Segmentation and Sales Coverage*

Thanks to its subscription model and long history of success, Pitney Bowes has acquired deep customer and industry data. It aggressively mines these data to segment customers and prospects, and give the sales force what Fruithandler termed "the right place to go and the right story to tell."

The mailing patterns and equipment usage of existing customers provide a basis for determining cross-selling and up-selling opportunities. Prospective customers can be analyzed based on existing customers of equivalent size and industry patterns. Fruithandler said:

> *We don't just throw our net out and try to catch anything. We know where to go for this product; we know where to go for that product.*

*We are constantly looking at our key segments and scoring cus-
tomers and prospects. Based on what industry you are in, what size
business you are, we can gauge whether you're a good prospect for
our core products or our additional applications. This gives the sales
reps a sharper focus on where they're going than just knocking on
all the doors. We try to guide them to the three doors that have a
greater likelihood of success.*

The sales organization began resegmenting customers "in the early
1990s," Fruithandler told us, "by taking the very top-end accounts in production mailers and putting them in a separate business unit to focus on
that piece of the market. It's the American Expresses of the world, highly
educated customers who understand mail is their cash flow and want to
know every ounce of what's going on. Somewhat simultaneous, we took
the low-end accounts, businesses with less than 25 employees, and put
them into a small-business-solutions segment that we handled through
direct mail, telesales, and later the Internet as the channels of choice." We
might well have mentioned this profitable application of sales analytics in
chapter 3, "Advance the Science of Sales and the Art of the Customer
Relationship, Part 1." It typifies how elite sales organizations maximize the
allocation of sales resources through rigorous experimentation.

With more recent pilot projects, the Pitney Bowes sales organization has
continued "to look at what's the next group of low-end accounts that we
can move into a telesales or other alternate channel." The results have been
so positive in terms of both customer satisfaction and revenue, that "over
the course of 10 years we've gone from 10 percent of our customer base
being managed by inside sales to 50 percent of our customer base being
managed by inside sales." This has freed the direct sales force to focus on
high-value solution selling to larger accounts, and to do so with both a
smaller head count and fewer accounts per rep. Over the same 10-year
period, Fruithandler noted, "the direct sales force has gone from managing
1.3 million customers to about 600,000 customers, and the number of sellers
has gone from a peak of around 2,500 to under 1,900. That's a big savings."

In addition to a direct outside sales force comprising both territory sales
reps and specialist sales reps focused on high-value products and services,
Pitney Bowes uses an independent dealer network and two inside sales
channels. The inside channels are telesales and Internet-sales for low-end
accounts and a retention telesales channel, a "save group" in Fruithandler's

words. "When customers say they don't want to do business with us anymore, before we go pick up the equipment, the retention channel gets on the phone and does a very decent job of keeping a lot of them."

Interestingly, the sales organization has adopted different mixes of these channels in the western and eastern parts of the United States. For Pitney Bowes, the west begins east of the Mississippi River in Tennessee and Indiana. This organizational alignment may seem to recall colonial times, when Ohio was "the Northwest frontier." No artifact of the past, however, this division reflects today's population densities.

In the eastern corridor, "the luxury of geographical population density" favors less inside sales and more outside sales, whereas from Indiana and Tennessee west there is a necessity for inside sales to handle a greater number of accounts. It is up to the head of sales in each area to decide exactly what channel mix is appropriate.

In the west, it did not make sense to have sales reps call on widely separated small accounts. Pitney Bowes therefore created an inside account management center in Spokane, WA. The first point of entry for the smaller accounts became the inside sales person. And if the needs of customers are such that this is not enough, they get referred to an outside sales person.

As Fruithandler explained:

> It's a question of deploying different degrees of the same coverage model. That was kind of a new thing for this company. We knew we needed to become more flexible because of regional differences in both population density and industry mix. In the sunbelt markets you have mostly service industries, not the blended manufacturing and financial services environment you have in the northeast. Fitting resources to customers in different regions requires a more sophisticated blending of the coverage models you utilize. The key is that at the end of the day, you unify everything by measuring results in terms of the same balanced scorecard.

Two more segmenting and coverage pilots we learned about in our conversations at Pitney Bowes particularly intrigued us. The first is "a competitive specialist pilot," which reflected the recognition, Fruithandler said, "that our sales force wasn't doing a real good job in calling on the competition's customers. So we carved out a small number of folks, and all they do is wake up every day and go after competitive meters."

One of Pitney Bowes's most successful sales experiments to date has been an "account-rotation pilot" that has been scaled up and made a regular practice. Having migrated low-end accounts to inside sales channels, the sales organization now rotates many of these accounts back to the outside sales force on a limited time basis. The accounts are selected based on lease renewal or on usage patterns that indicate the opportunity for selling additional products and services.

Fruithandler explained:

> *These are low-value, transactional accounts. Based on the marketing department's opportunity analysis, we rotate sets of 25,000 of them back to our field sales organization on a quarterly basis. Usually inside you'll get much higher hit rates, but lower average order size, than you will outside. But by rotating these selected accounts outside, we're getting higher hit rates and higher average order sizes. Our hit rate has doubled, our cancellation rate is flat, and our order size has improved by 30 percent.*

Because the accounts are rotated back to the inside sales channel at the end of the quarter, it motivates the outside sellers to maximize their temporary selling opportunities. And it ensures that over the long term the accounts are managed in the most cost-effective way by inside sellers.

## Learning from Successes and Failures

Through disciplined experimentation, the Pitney Bowes sales and marketing organization is proactively readying itself to adapt to the tumultuous changes that history shows inevitably confront every business, no matter how successful or long-lived it may be. As Fruithandler observed, "Many organizations react when their model is broken and they have to take drastic action to try to right it. We are looking forward while we still have a very good business model that is not broken."

That means having the willingness and creativity to learn from failures as well as successes. Fruithandler shared with us the story of "a sales specialization pilot where from a planning standpoint we thought we had a pretty good idea of what we wanted to do." The pilot put specialist salespeople in territories where they had no connection to existing accounts and were delegated solely to "conquest selling in smaller businesses."

Summing up the results, Fruithandler said, "It didn't work. We learned that if you want to put specialists in, you have to give them the right mix of customers. You need to give them some accounts where they have a greater likelihood of success. They need some customers who are going to renew existing applications, so that they are not out there doing all conquest selling. We deployed that learning in a subsequent pilot and it worked much better."

In this regard, Pitney Bowes has the courage to use its 75 U.S. sales districts as so many different laboratories for testing and fine-tuning sales innovations. "We manage each of those 75 locations on a balanced scorecard of sales results, revenue results, operational metrics, and human capital metrics," Fruithandler told us. "The most significant part of that is that it gives us 75 internal benchmarks. That's a pretty powerful weapon for seeing which operations and approaches are performing well and determining best practices."

The sales organization uses these benchmarks to keep redefining what constitutes success, continually raising the bar in terms of delivering value to customers, the company, and shareholders. At the time of our interviews, this ongoing effort was focusing sharply on customer retention. Fruithandler explained:

> One of the things a lot of sales organizations are guilty of is looking only at quota attainment. Quota attainment is nothing more than how well someone can negotiate with their boss. We want to look beyond quota attainment to organic revenue growth, market share, and controllable losses. What I mean by market share is when we consider all the products and services we offer, are we selling our fair share across the board or are we living on just one sure product? And what I mean by controllable losses is not only getting in and getting out with the sale, but maintaining the customer relationship. We're in the process now of redrafting our compensation plan, because it doesn't penalize you effectively for losing a customer.
>
> We sent that out on video to the sales force, calling it the redefinition of success. Previously success was attaining 150 percent of quota. Now we say, "Okay, Mr. or Ms. 150 percent of quota, let's look at your controllable losses. If you met or exceeded quota, but lost a valuable customer, that's not a good thing."

*If you lose customers, you lose your opportunity base. We need the sales organization to have a long-term view, versus a short-term, quarterly view of their compensation.*

The Pitney Bowes sales organization's commitment to keep striving for improvement is reflected clearly in its pilot programs. At the time of our interviews, there were 15 pilots under way at different stages in the direct sales force and several others in the inside sales force. As Rob Fruithandler put it, "We are always testing. Because the leadership of this company has made it clear that a victory is not a victory without a plan to grow on top of it."

## *Conclusion*

As the examples of Genzyme, Oracle, MasterCard, SAP Business Objects, Sony Electronics, and Pitney Bowes show, firms that want to achieve consistent profitability and growth must have sales organizations that embrace the need to experiment for both continuous improvement and game-changing transformations. One of the high-performing companies we highlight in this book, Xerox, offers a valuable perspective on the long-term benefit of this practice.

As Xerox's Mike MacDonald told us, the company's core competencies have traditionally been "great technology, great sales, and great service." Founded in 1906 as the Haloid Company, Xerox grew from a photographic paper business on the margins of Kodak's dominant market share to a giant in its own right, the leading player in the global copying machine industry that it founded with the game-changing innovation of xerography. That the brand name Xerox gave rise to the public's using the common name xerox for a copy made on any machine, just as the brand name Kleenex gave rise to the public's using the common name kleenex for any paper tissue, testifies to the firm's enormous success.

Attempts to expand and build on that success took the firm on a roller coaster ride throughout the 1970s, 1980s, and 1990s. In the 1970s, neglect of manufacturing efficiencies made Xerox vulnerable to low-cost Japanese manufacturers, and its share of the global plain-paper-copier market fell from 85 percent in 1974 to 40 percent in 1985. Diversification out of the core copier business was hit and miss: A successful hit with electronic typewriters, as the Xerox Memorywriter replaced the IBM Selectric as the typewriter of choice in many companies; a miss with personal computers, even though the famous Xerox Palo Alto Research Center (PARC) made the seminal breakthroughs in operating system architecture and user interface that would later be exploited by Apple; and an even costlier miss with a foray out of technology into insurance wholesaling.

In the 1990s, with career Xerox executive Paul Allaire as CEO and then chairman, the company shed its insurance business and battled back with market-leading color copiers and a focus on document processing in all its forms. Yet it almost snatched defeat from the jaws of victory with changes in sales organization ordered by Allaire's successor as CEO, Rick Thoman, who had been brought in to run the company after serving as CFO at IBM.

Thoman's changes were not creative experimentation but a command-and-control edict that overnight tried to shift the sales organization to operate by customer industry rather than by geographical location. The change made some sense logically in terms of specialized sales roles. But inflexibility, absence of trial and error, and lack of an effective transition plan proved disastrous.

After only 13 months, Thoman departed and was briefly replaced by his predecessor, Allaire, who remained the company's chairman. Allaire then led the Xerox board in choosing fellow Xerox lifer Anne Mulcahy, who had spent most of her career to that point in sales, to take over the reins. In the following years, Mulcahy — she soon succeeded Allaire as chairman as well as president and CEO — brought Xerox back from the brink with ceaseless effort and experimentation centered, in Mike MacDonald's words, around "great technology, great sales, and great service." Among the most significant elements in the turnaround was the sales organization's blending an evolving mix of generalist and specialist sales roles with a more cost-efficient geographical structure.

When Mulcahy took over the top job, Xerox had only $154 million in cash against $17.1 billion in debt. When she stepped down as CEO in 2009, naming company president Ursula Burns as her successor but remaining chairman of the board, Xerox had turned the red numbers black and then some, with $17.6 billion in revenue and $230 million in profit. The stage was set for Burns to add on to the company's core strength in document processing with the roughly $6 billion purchase of Affiliated Computer Services (ACS), the world's biggest business process outsourcing firm.

In a *New York Times* interview in March 2009, Mulcahy shared some of the lessons of the turnaround. Chief among them is the need for experimentation, or in Mulcahy's words, "adaptability and flexibility," on the part of an organization and all of its people. "One of the things that is mind-boggling right now," Mulcahy said, "is how much we have to change all the time … you have to embrace the ambiguity." As a result, she added, "You've got to give people permission to give you tough news, not shoot the messenger, thank people for identifying problems early and giving you the opportunity to solve them."

Every organization is bound to run into tough times, and sometimes the whole economy does. Recall MasterCard's Gary Flood's trenchant remark, "Challenging situations are bound to happen." But the sales organizations that have the courage and openness to make loud mistakes have a decided survival edge on those that don't.

## HOW GREAT SALES ORGANIZATIONS MAKE LOUD MISTAKES TO ACHIEVE CONTINUOUS IMPROVEMENT AND GAME-CHANGING TRANSFORMATIONS

### GREAT SALES ORGANIZATIONS:

- Always try to look around the corner to anticipate changes in customer needs and market conditions, and are always willing to change sales models and sales processes accordingly.
- Refine and discover best practices through frequent pilot projects using a fail-or-scale model.
- Create a nimble, cost-effective learning organization with a focus on "making loud mistakes" and "failing quickly."
- Hire people who are temperamentally suited to creative trial-and-error experimentation.
- Empower the sales force to succeed through failure by celebrating and rewarding learning from honest mistakes.
- Understand that the only unacceptable mistakes are those that are repeated.

# CHAPTER 6
# Live the Mission

**LEAD FROM THE FRONT; SPEAK CLEARLY** — and carry a big carrot; advance the science of sales and the art of the customer relationship; make loud mistakes — they're all ways for a sales organization to live its mission. Practically every firm these days has a mission statement centered around customers and their needs. Living the mission means walking the walk, not just talking the talk, of putting customers first and serving customers at a fundamental level.

One of the strongest common denominators we found among top sales organizations is an almost visceral belief in placing customers first and serving a customer-motivated mission. The exact nature of the mission depends on the firm's customers, but it invariably looks beyond quarterly and annual sales revenue and profit goals to the long-term interests of customers. Across companies as varied as FedEx, Genzyme, Honeywell Building Solutions, Johnson & Johnson, Johnson Controls, Oracle, SAP Business Objects, Sony Electronics, Thomson Reuters Legal, and Whirlpool, we saw how a noble purpose inspires elite sales organizations to achieve great performance.

The benefits of a sales organization's living the mission are that it:

- Builds credibility and trust with customers.

- Defeats commoditization and constitutes a powerful differentiator over competitors.

- Helps align resources with customer needs.

- Attracts the best sales talent, accelerates training and development, and motivates above-and-beyond-the-call-of-duty performance — "You can't inspire, unless you're inspired."

- Enhances innovation by increasing openness to new opportunities to serve customers profitably.

\* \* \*

# The Heart and Soul of a Sales Organization

Few companies put their beliefs into action as successfully as Johnson & Johnson (J&J). Not only is J&J the world's largest healthcare company and one of the most consistently profitable firms in any industry but it is also one of the world's most trusted brands. We had the opportunity to explore how the sales organizations for J&J's many businesses fulfill its customer-motivated purpose with Sue Petrella, J&J vice president for marketing and sales, and David Smith, vice president of global sales and marketing at J&J's eyecare subsidiary, Vistakon, maker of Acuvue disposable contact lenses. These executives shared insights, respectively, into the central role of sales in driving J&J's "$60 billion+ growth machine" and Vistakon's $2 billion+ contribution to that extraordinary enterprise.

J&J has enshrined its mission in what it calls its credo, one of the first and most explicit corporate mission statements. Originally written in 1943 by Robert Wood Johnson II, son and successor as CEO of company founder Robert Wood Johnson I, the credo sets forth J&J's belief in four responsibilities: First to caregivers, patients and their families, suppliers, and distributors; second to employees and their families; third to the company's home communities and the world; and fourth to stockholders.

The ranking of these constituencies is telling. So is the fact that as the face of the company to physicians and other customers in the healthcare industry, J&J's sales organizations bear the primary responsibility for fulfilling the credo. Admittedly, J&J formalized the credo after a successful existence of almost 40 years. It is no doubt easier for a financially strong company to say that its primary attention is on customer needs than for a firm that is battling for survival. But perhaps that is looking at things the wrong way round. Judging by what we heard at J&J, as well as reflecting on its extensive product line — over-the-counter and prescription products and medical devices and diagnostics — it is precisely its focus on customers that has driven J&J's long-running success for stockholders.

The company boasts an impressive list of medical sales firsts, from shortly after its founding in 1886 to the present: The first sterile surgical dressings and sutures, baby powder, dental floss, first-aid kits, ready-made bandages (the iconic Band-Aid), aspirin-free pain reliever (Tylenol), coronary artery stents, and, through Vistakon, disposable contact lenses — and this is by no means a complete list.

The mention of Tylenol is a reminder that in the autumn of 1982, when seven people in the Chicago area were murdered by a still unidentified person who added cyanide to Tylenol capsules, J&J quickly decided to pull more than $100 million worth of Tylenol products from store shelves throughout the United States. This sales action has deservedly become a landmark in corporate responsibility to consumers and a defining moment for all of J&J. At the time, J&J's leaders had no way of knowing that CEO James Burke's decision would ultimately allow the Tylenol brand not only to survive, but to thrive, because of the consumer trust it sustained and enhanced.

As of 2010, J&J had recorded 76 consecutive years of sales increases; 26 consecutive years of adjusted earnings increases; and 48 consecutive years of dividend increases. In addition, it has won regular recognition as one of the world's most trusted brands.

* * *

According to Sue Petrella, the credo is "the heart and soul of J&J, the way we create and build businesses that improve people's lives." A key word is "businesses." Petrella stressed that this "is not altruism." Rather, the credo expresses J&J's faith that a win–win business ethos will carry it through good times and bad.

J&J is not the only firm in our sample of high-performing sales organizations where a customer focus is central to the firm's functioning and not merely superficial wordsmithing by corporate public relations. Similarly, at bioengineering firm Genzyme, a motto of longtime CEO Henri Termeer guides the company and its sales organization: "Good medicine is good business."

But as we've already pointed out, it is not just healthcare companies where there is a strong connection between a larger mission and exceptional business performance. For Honeywell Building Solutions and Johnson Controls, for example, "green" initiatives are not just a slogan but an increasingly important factor in winning new contracts and motivating salespeople.

Notwithstanding its hyper-competitive reputation, the Oracle sales organization recognizes the importance of customer needs. In the words of Keith Block, executive vice president of North American sales, either "every sale, you're solving a customer problem," or "the organization fails, the company fails, customers fail" (see chapter 1, "Lead from the Front").

At Sony Electronics, Ken Stevens said that consumers "trust us with their downtime .... If we do anything that jeopardizes that, it's an enormous responsibility on our side." Likewise, home appliance leader Whirlpool has sustained a premium price advantage, when most competitors have resigned themselves to commoditization, by looking beyond product features to end-user benefits and values. Whirlpool understands that its purpose is not simply making and selling appliances but making and selling appliances that suit the lifestyles of today's consumers. In addition to this sharp focus on serving end-consumers, both Sony and Whirlpool have broadened their missions by predicating their sales organizations' success on the success of their retail partners. Each of these firms reaps consistent growth by growing the entire category in which it operates (see chapter 4, "Advance the Science of Sales and the Art of the Customer Relationship, Part 2").

Greg Lorden, senior vice president and general manager of SAP Business Objects, a leading provider of performance management software and business intelligence, described a larger mission as "the beginning of credibility and trust." He explained how "a vision that goes beyond the quarterly sales number" has propelled Business Objects since its founding as an independent company in France in 1990 (acquired by SAP in 2007):

> When I joined the sales organization in 1995, most customers in the United States didn't know who we were and we were coming in two steps behind IBM. But we cast a vision that was more than the bottom line, and that enabled us to reach beyond what we had.
>
> After a sale I often asked customers, "Why did you buy from us?" They more or less always said, "You came in here, you listened, and you made us think."
>
> Again, it's the beginning of credibility. Whether you're selling business intelligence or servers or insurance plans for 401(k)s, customers don't want to become experts in those things. They want somebody they can trust to deliver value for them.

When a sales organization clearly demonstrates to customers that it has a customer-motivated mission, price is no longer the most important issue. "Making the sale is tying together need, money, and trust," Lorden said. "If the need is there and we build the credibility, the trust piece, customers almost always find the money."

Greg Lorden also trenchantly observed that "the mission statements of all companies look alike. They all talk about integrity and investing in employees and communities. The trick is making it real." That requires "translating the high-level strategy into the daily tactics of the sales rep in Milwaukee or wherever. There has to be alignment and accountability to a vision that goes beyond the quota."

With that in mind, let's look at how the J&J credo is, in Sue Petrella's words, "operationalized on a daily basis" by its sales organizations.

## *Aligning Sales Resources with a Larger Mission*

Having started her J&J career as a trainee sales rep and risen to run several of its sales organizations, Sue Petrella is well placed to describe how the company aligns sales resources with customer needs and in so doing sets itself apart from the competition. Again, the chief difference maker, Petrella said, is "a passionate belief in the credo; everything cascades from there." The "connectedness of the sales force to the credo ... [promotes] a stickiness to the customer ... [and] an ability to romance products," either for market launch or to counter "fast followers'" efforts to commoditize them.

To assess the fulfillment of its larger mission as spelled out in the credo, every second year J&J surveys all of its employees around the world, currently about 120,000 people, "from janitors to C-suite executives" at company, division, and corporate headquarters. Insisting on internal transparency, J&J publishes the survey results, "the good, the bad, and the ugly," throughout the company and makes a point of acknowledging its failures and addressing any shortfalls in living up to the credo. In the period between surveys, J&J engages in more limited "pulse-taking" on the larger mission, typically at the division or subsidiary company level.

For the sales force, it bears repeating that living the credo above all involves what Petrella called "a stickiness to the customer." In the case of physicians, this begins with both branded and non-branded outreach when they are completing their medical studies. J&J takes pains to see that sales reps "learn to speak the language of medicine" in general and in terms of specialties and subspecialties served by specific product sets, such as minimally invasive surgery or the treatment of cardiac arrhythmias.

Like their counterparts at other high-performing sales organizations in different industries, J&J's sellers must possess and wield considerable intellectual capital. Indeed, J&J sales reps must often speak the language of medicine fluently enough to teach physicians new medical techniques and procedures. At the same time, the sales reps must appreciate the perspective of patients, making common cause with physicians to improve patient outcomes.

Understanding medical issues from both physician and patient perspectives, in tandem with the innovations produced by J&J's robust R&D or secured from outside through acquisition, enables sales reps to "romance their products," including those that may seem indistinguishable from products sold by competitors, often at lower prices. Within Sue Petrella's own J&J experience, that tradition embraces her early colleagues, sales reps who "could romance silk thread on a needle" and "sell gauze at a premium price that doctors would pay for out of their own pockets," because its quality and softness were better for patients.

Petrella continued, "I love that about J&J, that belief that even your undifferentiated product can be clearly differentiated, and you'll be darned if anybody's going to tell you differently. That's selling."

Some of those same sales reps are still with J&J, Petrella noted, but instead of gauze (now an unprofitable commodity as prices have fallen), "they're largely in our medical device companies." Although they are in the latter stages of their careers, their belief in the J&J credo makes them "the best salespeople in the world."

Passionate belief in J&J's larger mission, Petrella maintained, drives such major J&J successes as Biosense Webster, maker of electrophysiology products for controlling cardiac arrhythmias; Ethicon Endo-Surgery, a $2 billion business that pioneered and has the largest share in the fast-growing minimally invasive surgery market; and Cordis, the first entrant in the cardiac stent market.

Petrella said:

> *In medical devices you definitely have a product you can romance. You have something that you can touch and feel. You have the camaraderie that you can build with physician customers by showing them a new clinical technique and teaching it to them. You create a relationship around the mutual goal of making things better for the patient.*

*At Ethicon Endo-Surgery, wow, it was just really exciting taking that from a $200 million opportunity to a $2 billion opportunity roughly 14 years later. But the money's not what got shouted about here. We created a market. We helped surgeons do laparoscopic procedures in a way that got you home in two days, and back to work in two weeks, versus being in bed for six to eight weeks. And that's really what the mission is all about.*

\* \* \*

All healthcare companies espouse a patient-motivated mission. As already mentioned, Genzyme CEO Henri Termeer's watchword is, "Good medicine is good business." But like J&J, Genzyme recognizes that making its motto real requires daily action. Dan Regan, Genzyme Renal's head of sales, told us that he had to "ensure that the rep in Toledo, OH, or in St. Paul, MN, knows what our mission is, and that we have that consistency across the country as we expand as a sales organization. That definitely keeps me up at night, knowing that I want to keep this culture."

Accountability to Genzyme's customer-motivated mission thus functions, Regan said, as "a kind of managerial control consistency." His colleague Joe Brennan, Genzyme Biosurgery's head of sales, spoke to the same point, noting that alignment with the mission begins with corporate leadership:

*One product I am responsible for, Epicel, has a four-person sales force. If someone has a catastrophic burn and the doctors can't skin graft them, a stamp-sized piece of their skin is sent to us and we grow skin for them. A sugar factory near Atlanta, GA blew up a while ago, and a lot of the victims of that got our product.*

*It's a life-saving product, but we don't make much money on it because we don't sell that much of it.*

*Genzyme has an award called the Alpine Award, with the winner selected by the CEO. It usually goes to one sales or marketing team and one sales rep in the organization. The Epicel team won it a few years ago, and an Epicel rep just won it. Four people, $8 million in revenue. That's in the context of almost $4 billion in total company sales revenue.*

*It says a lot about our CEO, and about what Genzyme wants to do, that the award goes to great sales and marketing of a product with insignificant revenue.*

The cynic may say that customer-focused missions are easy to develop in healthcare companies, but most of us are not in the business of saving lives. Developing the mission may be less straightforward in other industries, but our research tells us that accountability to a larger mission is critically important regardless of the product or market. Accountability to the customer is a chain that begins with company and sales leadership, and links all of a sales organization's actions.

FedEx sales leaders Dave Edmonds and Tom Schmitt talked to us about the rigor required to fulfill the company's "broader mission [of] enhancing customers' efficiency." Dave Edmonds said, "That's why your value quantification has got to be sharp. Because you're not going to go to a CFO and lay out a comparison to an income statement and balance sheet, and expect to win the deal, unless you have bulletproof numbers."

A sales organization's accountability to a larger mission emerges very clearly in its hiring and training as well as its ethical standards. As we shall see, that is true not only in healthcare companies but across the business landscape in firms as diverse as SAP Business Products, Johnson Controls, Oracle, and Thomson Reuters Legal.

## Hiring and Training to Fulfill a Larger Mission

One of the most important areas for making the larger mission a reality is in hiring and training both sales reps and first-line sales managers. J&J's effort to sustain its salespeople's fervent belief in the credo led Sue Petrella to reflect on how the company handles hiring, training, and career advancement. She began by observing that doctors in many medical specialties remain largely all white and all male:

*A great example is electrophysiology, the specialty served by Biosense Webster. Almost 100 percent of electrophysiologists are white men, so it's easy to say, "Well, we want them to be comfortable with our sales reps, so that's who we're going to recruit." It's a mistake. You're missing out on the creative aspect of what people bring to the table that makes your company better. A lot of companies don't get it. J&J gets it.*

*J&J's really been great at making sure that the population of your sales force reflects the diversity of the patients that you serve as well as the physicians you call on.*

*Biosense Webster is an example of that. They had me as a female sales leader replaced by an Hispanic male. The sales force is immensely diverse not only in terms of gender and ethnicity, but also backgrounds, and it is one of the fastest growing, most successful companies at J&J.*

J&J implicitly recognizes that physician demographics are not set in stone and that over time the makeup of more and more specialties will reflect the diversity of the general population. The competitors whose sales forces mirror the demographics of various physician groups as they now exist should ask themselves whether they will be able to keep pace with that change. J&J is ahead of the curve.

Recall the similar observation of Whirlpool's Sam Abdelnour (see chapter 4, "Advance the Science of Sales and the Art of the Customer Relationship, Part 2") that his very successful, but aging and homogenous, sales force had to change to reflect the increasing diversity of the population. The point of this demographic evolution for Whirlpool, as for J&J, is not altruism. It is the business value a firm derives from a sales organization in tune with the needs of end-consumers.

Regarding the training of sales reps, Sue Petrella boasted, "We have the best training of anybody in the industry. We're known for it."

Fresh hires receive an average of 8 to 10 weeks of training, including "general sales skills as well as specific technical training. In every sales job at J&J, there's a specific technical competency. You go to work for Biosense Webster, you have to learn electrophysiology. Boy, is it hard."

The training comprises both distance and classroom learning. Although J&J appreciates the cost benefits of distance learning, it also insists on bringing people face-to-face with the best teachers it can find in order to achieve a level of technical competency that goes beyond the competition. Sue Petrella cited Aaron Ruhalter, M.D., professor of anatomy and surgery at the University of Cincinnati College of Medicine and executive director of medical education for J&J's Endo-Surgery Institute, "who has taught every single sales rep at Ethicon Endo-Surgery; he's touched every single one, without exception, since 1985."

J&J sees sales training as having two purposes, not only imparting skills and knowledge but also building esprit de corps. So it also wants to bring new hires face-to-face with each other in order to forge bonds and reinforce a mutual belief in the credo.

Petrella said:

> *You can save a lot of money with distance e-learning. But bringing people together in the classroom and other settings creates bonds and loyalty. If you teach the skills, but you don't instill that belief and loyalty, you've just created some really great talent for someone else.*

At J&J, training does not end after 8 to 10 weeks but is career-long. That's "a big part of the next key piece of a successful organization, the ongoing care and feeding of your people. It's a lot of investment."

All J&J employees have access to "a consortium of courses" on business and more general topics, such as "being an effective listener." In addition, J&J offers a suite of tools and courses for managers, a "leadership roadmap."

Petrella explained:

> *A tremendous effort is put into developing management competence. So coaching and counseling, recruiting, how to give feedback, how you value people, how you treat them and talk to them. It's technical management competency, but more than that it's ... how you model the credo.*

Echoing her "this is not altruism" comment early on in our conversation, Petrella also emphasized the importance of "making sure that the financial incentives are aligned, so that people feel rewarded for the job that they do."

This does not mean that J&J necessarily pays top dollar in the industry. J&J salespeople can do very well financially, "but we're not hanging on to our people because we pay them the biggest gobs of money. That's not our strongest suit." Instead, Petrella believes, it is the total package of direct and indirect benefits of working at J&J that sustains the excellence of the sales force and keeps its retention rate high. That is something to ponder for cost-conscious business leaders everywhere.

Other top-performing companies in our survey have already taken this to heart. For example, Kim Metcalf-Kupres, vice president for sales and marketing at Johnson Control's battery division, Power Solutions, shared with us that "the vision of safe, sustainable products is ... something that resonates with our salespeople. It's one of the things that really attracts people to work here."

Speaking both for himself and his organization, SAP Business Object's Greg Lorden said that "if you're just in business to make the quarter's or the year's numbers, you're vulnerable to losing your best people. If I didn't have a long-term vision for building the best, the highest integrity, software sales organization, I would have quit six times by now myself."

Without discounting the importance of financial compensation, Lorden observed that there is also a strong human need to have a positive impact:

> *You can't inspire unless you're inspired. It's very important to be aligned with the passion to have a positive impact. My wife recently told me, "I've never seen you have so much energy." We have four young children, and I come home with energy to play. That's from the opportunity to make an impact where people can build great sales skills, doing it the right way with integrity.*
>
> *The key is you've got to have a vision that goes beyond the sales number, and it's got to be aligned in action every day.*

Oracle's Keith Block likewise told us that an effective seller can't be solely "coin operated," but must have a sense of working for the "greater cause" of helping the company and its customers to thrive (see chapter 1, "Lead from the Front").

To illustrate how "sales at Genzyme Renal is a passion," Dan Regan pointed to a successful sales rep who has become an equally effective sales manager and to similar behavior throughout the sales organization:

> *Todd was a sales rep for seven years and he was Genzyme Renal's number-one rep, or in what we call our Summit Club category, probably six out of those seven years. Todd woke up every morning and told his wife, "I'm going to save some patients' lives."*
>
> *One of the parts of Genzyme's culture is to relay the experiences of patients. It's not uncommon for somebody to be giving a presentation and read a letter from a patient about the positive impact that our drugs have had on that person's life.*

For the larger mission to be fully realized, Regan added, concern for the customer has to be reflected in concern for employees and open communication. His colleague Joe Brennan addressed the need for a balance in demanding great performance from sales reps and supporting their efforts to achieve: "If someone has something going on at home, that always takes precedence and that's a great way to gain loyalty. By the same token, if someone steps across a line, there will be ramifications and repercussions."

Illustrating the extent to which the larger mission is embedded in the Genzyme culture, the repercussions may come from fellow sales reps. When "a rep stepped out of line at a sales meeting," Brennan said, it was another rep who told him, "That doesn't happen here."

## A Larger Mission and Ethical Behavior

The toughest challenge to maintaining a customer-motivated mission is when there are ethical quandaries. In one form or another, every sales organization faces them from time to time.

Summing up the "care and feeding of your people," Petrella said, "They're your employees. You've got to love them and invest in them. It's the whole second paragraph of the credo." This does not mean anything goes, however; far from it. "I don't want to suggest that J&J is perfect, because there's going to be crime in a city of 120,000. But you know what? Unethical behavior is not tolerated, even if it led to tremendous success. It just isn't. That's part of the culture. That's how you build loyalty. And at the end of the day, it's because of these things in the credo that you have this incredible profit performance of J&J over time."

At Thomson Reuters Legal, which provides workflow solutions to legal, intellectual property, compliance, business and government professionals, Michael Orrick made a similar observation. "Ethics in an industry like this is critical," he said. Thomson Reuters Legal's sales organization has to balance "a very high ethical standard … [with] a very strong achievement orientation …. Our customers shop from just a few select vendors, so we can't afford to be driving customers away; we have to ensure that the ethical and quality standards in our business are always in front of our minds."

For Genzyme's Dan Regan, the ethics of the company rest in the sales reps' hands. This means that in hiring new sales reps, "first and foremost, we're looking for good people." Regan elaborated:

*The sales reps are out there on their own so much. They're probably driving around in their cars by themselves 28 out of 30 days.*

*They're the face of the company. The rep walks into the doctor's office, and the doctor doesn't care who our CEO is; he doesn't care who Dan Regan is. All he knows is that the rep's walking in the door, and that's Genzyme.*

*So we need to make sure that we have somebody who is a good person who's going to make good decisions, and when faced with the right thing to do, the wrong thing to do, or something in the middle, will do the right thing.*

*I think you keep people accountable first and foremost by hiring the right people."*

## Living the Mission at Vistakon

After Sue Petrella's overview of how J&J sales organizations not only talk the credo talk, but also walk the credo walk, we wondered how J&J's larger mission shapes behavior inside one of its operating companies. We got our answer in a detailed conversation with David Smith, head of sales at Vistakon, whose Acuvue brand was the first disposable contact lens and continues to hold leading market share.

In our conversation at Vistakon's headquarters in Jacksonville, FL, we focused on the U.S. sales organization. This conversation, which occurred some months after our talk with Sue Petrella, did not explicitly focus on the J&J credo. But in a sign of the credo's importance throughout J&J, there were implicit echoes of it in everything David Smith told us.

\* \* \*

Like other J&J medical products, Vistakon's Acuvue brand disposable contact lenses must meet the needs of two sets of customers, the eyecare professionals who prescribe them and the consumers who wear them. The wrinkle is that disposable contact lenses "are a medical device where doctors make money directly off of selling the product."

Echoing Sue Petrella, David Smith emphasized above all the Vistakon sales organization's belief in the value of disposable lenses to both doctors and patients. Smith explained that, in the beginning, it was not an easy sell:

*No one thought this idea of throwing lenses away was going to fly. Doctors were really skeptical. They said they weren't going to be able to do good follow-up with their patients, that the lenses were too expensive and people wouldn't throw them away after a week and would try to make them last. There was huge initial skepticism. In fact, after the first test market in mid-1987 in Florida, J&J came within a hair of just canning the whole thing.*

Recruited from Procter & Gamble to join the fledgling operation, Smith recalled that "the sales training was unique in my experience, because the first half of the first day was spent on one concept, belief in the J&J credo."

Following the first test market, Vistakon decided to give away diagnostic lenses to doctors, "so they could put them on as many eyes as they could." Then in early 1988 the entire field sales force, "only 30 sales reps, all got on a bus in California for the second test market. And they went up and down the coast doing nothing but preaching that disposable lenses were the way to go." This was a success, and "that flipped the switch. We went from 30 sales reps in January 1988 to 150 by July."

In spirited competition with Bausch & Lomb, the contact-lens market leader and fast follower with disposable contact lenses, Vistakon won leading market share. Within three years, it became "number one in the overall contact lens market." Despite this success, Smith said, "It didn't feel like we were growing as fast as we were. We probably talked about belief all the time for the first five years."

The overwhelming majority of disposable contact lens sales — "90 percent of our business" — is through doctors of optometry. At the time of product launch, that meant mostly small "mom-and-pop" operations. Speaking about the "stickiness to the customer" that Sue Petrella told us characterized all of J&J's sales organizations, David Smith said, "We knew we had to get really close to the optometrists, because we were the newcomers coming in with a new product. And we could be enthusiastic and passionate, but we couldn't be arrogant, because optometrists are kind of salt-of-the-earth people who really care about their patients."

Below we'll explore the Vistakon sales organization's need to balance "patient issues" and optometrists' "practice issues." But the latter concern was complicated because the "mom-and-pop" optometrists could not keep the disposable contact lens business to themselves. Large retailers such as Walmart and Costco also soon offered disposable contact lenses in optical departments staffed by salaried optometrists. And before long

Internet and mail-order vendors appeared. Currently, David Smith told us, Vistakon's business is about 45 percent through independent optometrists, 45 percent through large retailers, and about 10 percent through Internet and mail-order vendors.

However, for several years, Vistakon put its larger mission ahead of short-term revenues and refused to sell its disposable lenses to Internet and mail-order vendors on ethical grounds. Smith explained, "Into the early 2000s, we didn't sell to those folks, because they weren't following prescription laws. We made heroic efforts to keep our products out of gray market channels." The situation changed in 2003, after Congress passed a new federal law, the Fairness to Contact Lens Consumers Act, and the Internet and mail-order vendors "agreed to follow the prescription laws and to verify prescriptions with doctors."

Intent on living its larger mission, Vistakon worked to support independent optometrists in adjusting to competition from big retailers and the Internet and mail order. The guiding principle was to serve both direct customers, the prescribing optometrists and end-consumers.

In this connection, David Smith spoke about how he wants Vistakon's sales reps to measure the success of a sales call. The goal is not to sell "X number of boxes of lenses," but, inspired by a belief in the superior quality, safety, comfort, and overall value of Vistakon's products, to effect "a practice change by the optometrist that gets more people wearing Acuvue disposable lenses at the end of the day."

Vistakon does extensive direct-to-consumer marketing and advertising. But as Smith explained:

> *In consumer products, the consumer sees an ad, gets off the couch, goes to the store, goes to the shelf, and picks up the product. In our business, the consumer sees the ad, then has to call the doctor to get an appointment, and when they get to the shelf, there is no shelf. There is a person in a white coat saying, "I know you saw the Acuvue commercial, but I'm going to tell you what you really need." So our sales reps have to be able to affect that person in the white coat. Otherwise all of this great consumer advertising is for nothing. The measure of success at the end of the sales call is that the rep walks out and knows that the doctor is going to change his or her practice behavior.*

The upshot is that every sales call has two sets of messages. Smith said, "We are talking to the doctor first about all the directional reasons to use our products: Safety, efficacy and effectiveness, price. Then, for example, we have to stop and say, 'By the way, it's back-to-school time, and you know teens are the entry point of contact lens wearing. Let's talk through the practice elements that will keep those patients in your practice."

When vendors offering contact lenses via the Internet and mail order started following the prescription laws, the independent brick-and-mortar optometrists "wanted us to insulate them from competition, and we weren't going to do that." But by sharing Vistakon's understanding of consumer preferences and behaviors with the optometrists, the sales reps helped "doctors adjust to the fact that that's reality. And they got better at offering the things that the patient would walk away from them for not having. They got better at convenience, they got better at pricing, they got better at servicing their lenses. Actually price wasn't that big of a deal. It was mostly about convenience and home delivery and not having to circle back all the time to the doctor's office."

It's worth noting that Vistakon also shares its consumer understanding with the prescription eyewear departments of big retailers. "We are doing a lot more ethnographic research," Smith told us, "to understand what happens when somebody is walking around a Walmart store, for example, and sees the optical department. Why do they or don't they walk into that department? What are they thinking? The buying process for someone who is new to contact lenses has a lot of hurdles and off-ramps. We share those insights with our salespeople, and they in turn share them with their accounts."

In selling its products through multiple channels, Vistakon also pays great attention to what Sue Petrella called "the ongoing care and feeding of" employees. This concern points to how the Vistakon sales organization's pursuit of a larger mission follows the J&J credo in linking its responsibility to customers with its responsibility to employees. David Smith told us that Vistakon sales reps are "channel independent" when it comes to sales credit. In addition to commission credit for sales through local optometrists, eyewear chains (like LensCrafters), and the big retail optical departments, they also "get direct credit for lenses purchased through an Internet or mail order channel by patients who live in their territory."

Vistakon sales reps are also channel independent, so to speak, in their access to advancement within the organization. A telesales group handles accounts that cannot be serviced effectively by field sales reps for reasons of geography or size. Telesales and field sales reps do not share accounts, but for the last few years recent hires in both groups have participated in "what we call the SLDP, our Sales Leadership Development Program." This program begins with telesales, which has been transformed from a backwater into a feeder pool for talent development. Smith explained:

> *Typically we would hire someone with three to four years of experience in some other industry. About five years ago we made a decision to grow our own, because we were getting pretty good sales reps, but we weren't getting good future sales managers.*

> *So we said we are going to go on campus, we are going to get real competitive on salary, we are going to recruit heavily, we are going to get the best people out of the best colleges, and we are going to bring them down here for daily competition with other really strong young college grads. And two years later we have great field sales reps that we can spin out to anywhere in the country.*

> *While we're on campus we are adamant about saying, "We are not hiring sales reps. We are hiring our future sales managers and our future business leaders. It just so happens that your first couple of jobs are going to be as a telesales rep and then a field sales rep. We can't tell you how quickly you can get to sales manager or district manager or regional manager, or into marketing or general management. But the best place to start in a company like ours is with the customer."*

Training and career development at Vistakon occur in what Smith termed "a feedback-rich environment." Because the feedback is "so constant, people get used to it," and if it is not forthcoming for some reason, "they will say, 'Hey, wait a minute, where is my feedback? What did I do right? What can I improve on?'"

In common with all the high-performing customer-motivated companies in our research, Vistakon constantly strives to improve the quality and quantity of coaching by sales managers. Smith said:

> *We have done a lot of analysis, and the key thing that differentiates whether we are moving our entire sales force, moving the entire performance bell curve over, is our coaching. The most important person in our company is the first-line sales manager. We constantly ask, are we finding ways to get them from three days of coaching a*

*week to four? Are we removing barriers to increase that coaching time? And are we investing to make sure that the coaching is good?*

*The underpinnings of our culture are focused on belief and passion, on deep empathy with our customers and how they act and how we need to act with them, and on a coaching- and feedback-rich environment for our employees.*

An area that exemplifies Vistakon's stickiness in serving a larger, customer-motivated mission, along with its respect for employees and concern for their development, is the interaction of sales, marketing, and sales analytics. David Smith told us that Vistakon ensures "cross-pollination" of sales and marketing by "aggressively" rotating members of each group through other functions, and by staffing a recently beefed up sales analytics group with "ex-sales guys who have a real problem-solving and analytical bent."

Sales and marketing are accountable for four shared metrics: "sales growth, sales share, messaging, — which means are we communicating effectively to customers, and customer satisfaction, which we are now doing more in the area of Net Promoter Scores." Net Promoter Score is a customer loyalty metric calculated by taking the percentage of customers who would recommend the firm (promoters) and subtracting the percentage of customers who would not (detractors.)

Vistakon regularly brings sales and marketing people together on its Marketing Advisory Panel (MAP), which "started as a way for sales reps to give input to marketing on what sales aids should look like." Before decisions are made, MAP does focus groups with doctors to ensure that customer needs drive its activities.

Smith pointed to sales analytics as one of the biggest recent contributions to putting customer needs first and serving them effectively. He explained:

*Sales analytics is something we finally started getting right a few years ago. We did not have a separate sales analytics group. We had sales admin, and sales admin produced a lot of reports. But we were producing reports; we weren't producing insight. We were producing data; we weren't producing information and knowledge.*

*So in 2004 we finally dedicated the headcount and the money and the resources, and we established a sales analytics group that has really made a ton of difference. Now our sales reps spend a heck of a lot less time reading reports and more time looking at insights.*

The sales analytics group's most important set of insights resulted in a new four-category segmentation of optometrists. "We had never done any kind of formal segmentation," Smith said. "We found that the most meaningful way to segment our customers was based on their loyalty, their sales, and their openness to innovation and new products. We discovered we basically have four groups: Loyal innovators, loyal conservatives, competitive innovators, and competitive conservatives. And we defined eight Accepted Practice Beliefs, or APBs, for each segment."

In Vistakon's early years, new product launches were few and far between. After Vistakon brought the first disposable contact lenses to market in 1987, it introduced its second, third, and fourth products, respectively, in 1991, 1995, and 1998. But since 2000, Vistakon's R&D efforts have been bearing an increasing amount of fruit and the company has launched an average of two new products a year. Today the Acuvue product line includes daily disposable lenses, lenses that can be slept in, bifocal lenses, astigmatism-correcting lenses, and cosmetic lenses, and the formulation of the lenses is constantly being refined.

The new segmentation has proven the value of having a larger, customer-motivated mission by contributing to effective product launches. Thanks to a deeper understanding of customer and consumer need, Vistakon has enhanced its ability to discuss both practice and patient issues with optometrists. Instead of a single sales aid for a product or sales initiative, Vistakon now develops four color-coded sales aids for the four optometrist segments.

There were bumps along the road as the sales organization tried to base its actions on the new customer segments and tell the right story to the right customer. "Marketing would come up with one great story," Smith said, "and typically it was the story that loyal innovators wanted to hear." The sales organization had to push back and say, "This is a great sales aid for the loyal innovator, but we need some help in these other quadrants."

A nifty side benefit is that the new segmentation has also improved coaching. Smith explained:

> Before this segmentation, the sales manager went on a sales call with a rep and said, "Okay, what are we going to do on the call? We're going to sell a lot more boxes. Let's go do it."
>
> Now it's, "Okay, this guy is a loyal innovator, we're pretty sure that's accurate. And here is the status of his business with us. So based on

*his being a loyal innovator and how he likes to make decisions, and based on where he currently is from an order standpoint, here is the sales aid we are going to use. And while we're on the call, let's keep in mind this coaching area that we agreed on."*

*That's a very different coaching experience than saying, "Let's go in and sell more boxes."*

Vistakon's ability to strengthen customer relationships and better serve customer needs, via more precise segmentation, clearly ties into its larger mission. So, too, does Vistakon's concern for long-range planning. It assembles and continually updates near-, medium-, and long-range Plans of Action (POAs). Smith elaborated:

*The Plan of Action process starts with the customer and reaches back to the product development group. The sales reps receive a quarterly POA, but every year we are working on three cycles: POA 1, POA 2, and POA 3. The basic macro concepts are set through the following year, and the product launches are set through the following two years.*

*With our sales VPs in our different regions we are looking three to five years out to ask three questions. What products are going to come in? What products are going to go out? And what sales efforts and resources are we going to have to apply to all of that?"*

\* \* \*

Sue Petrella spoke to us about J&J's "non-branded" activities in outreach to physicians and other caregivers and in continuing medical education. In this spirit, Vistakon and its parent created the Johnson & Johnson Vision Care Institute (VCI) with a main campus near Vistakon's headquarters in Jacksonville, FL; domestic satellite locations affiliated with the New England College of Optometry in Boston, MA, and the Pennsylvania College of Optometry in Elkins Park, PA; and international satellite locations in Brazil, China, the Czech Republic, Dubai, South Korea, Taiwan, and Thailand.

The U.S. locations have hosted students from all nineteen North American schools and colleges of optometry. David Smith said:

*We had talked about it for years, then a few years ago we finally stepped up to the plate to make a commitment to our customers' long-*

*term professional education. The Vision Care Institute is set up to be non-branded, non-product specific. It's all about doctor education, with seminars in skill training and specialty contact lens fitting that supplement and complement the curriculum in optometry schools.*

The seminars include practice development as well as purely medical matters. Indeed, the VCI has mounted a "Chief Executive Optometrist" initiative with the University of Pennsylvania's Wharton School, designed to help optometrists maximize their practices' earning potential.

One might argue that only a hugely successful company like J&J could afford to make such large investments in customer outreach without direct brand benefit, or that the J&J brand is never entirely out of view in the company's long history of similar efforts. But remember Sue Petrella's words about the J&J credo: "This is not altruism. This is a business," whose win–win ethos has produced an "incredible profit performance ... over time."

## *Conclusion*

J&J's credo, its belief in a mission larger than its own agenda, has inspired it and its operating companies, including Vistakon, to achieve enormous success. For Vistakon, that has meant reaching $2 billion in annual sales within twenty years of its 1987 startup.

J&J is not alone in recognizing the power of a customer-motivated mission. Belief in a mission larger than the company also energizes the other high-performing sales organizations in our sample, such as FedEx, Genzyme, Honeywell Building Solutions, Johnson Controls, Oracle, Sony Electronics, Thomson Reuters Legal, and Whirlpool, among others.

SAP Business Objects' vision of a mission beyond the quarterly and annual sales numbers led to record-breaking sales. Greg Lorden happily announced to his sales organization, "Ladies and gentlemen, we have an unbalanced scorecard. We have just done phenomenally."

In the remarkable turnaround at Honeywell Building Solutions (see chapter 2, "Speak Clearly — and Carry a Big Carrot"), the sales organization found tremendous motivation in the larger mission of saving the division. The excitement of this mission even attracted back sales talent that had left the company in its down years. And Johnson Controls leveraged its larger mission to win the contract to supply all the batteries for Ford's hybrid-engine cars.

The larger missions of Sony Electronics and Whirlpool have contributed substantially to their maintaining leadership positions within their trade retail customers and end-consumers alike, despite an economy-wide downturn that hit both the consumer electronics and home appliance categories brutally hard (see chapter 4, "Advance the Science of Sales and the Art of the Customer Relationship, Part 2").

A larger mission is not a panacea. As we have also seen, it must be actualized day-by-day. But it is an essential factor in great sales organization and company-wide performance.

One of the most powerful advantages of a customer-motivated mission is that it helps keep a firm nimble, ready to spot and seize new opportunities. Vistakon's David Smith told us, "We started off as a contact lens company. But our mission is all about eye and vision care. Our official name in most countries is Johnson & Johnson Vision Care. We have a small pharmaceutical division, and we are keeping our eye out for other opportunities." The sales organization plays a significant role in opportunity identification thanks to its continually striving for better understanding of both its direct customers and end-consumers. There may or may not be a pun intended in Vistakon's "keeping an eye out," but there is no question that such perspectives are a hallmark of a larger mission and of sales excellence in general.

## WHY GREAT SALES ORGANIZATIONS LIVE THE MISSION

- Builds credibility and trust with customers.
- Defeats commoditization and constitutes a powerful differentiator over competitors.
- Aids alignment of resources with customer needs.
- Attracts the best sales talent, accelerates its training and development, and motivates above-and-beyond-the-call-of-duty performance — "You can't inspire unless you're inspired."
- Enhances innovation by increasing openness to new opportunities to serve customers profitably.

# CHAPTER 7
# Sales-Added Value: The New Model for Great Sales Organizations — and Great Corporations

**THERE WAS A TIME WHEN SALES COULD NOT HOLD ITS HEAD UP** and look "core business functions" — marketing, finance, research and development, or manufacturing — in the eye. Nothing ever happened for a firm until it reached a customer, persuaded the customer that it had something of value to offer, and exchanged that something for the customer's hard earned cash. Nothing happened, and nobody got paid, until a sale occurred. The sales organization linked the customer and the firm, and made the sale. But sales got little respect for its efforts.

As we hope this book has demonstrated, that familiar tale, if it were ever true, now lacks all validity. Today's most successful enterprises value sales as a core function, the equal of all the other business functions — from marketing to manufacturing, and even finance.

The modern sales organization wields influence in step with the intellectual capital it acquires and extends in order to serve as the interface between a firm and its customers. Today's high-performing sales organization does five things well. It takes the lead in creating and delivering customer value; it builds and sustains a customer-motivated culture that inspires and empowers the sales force, and the firm as a whole, to excel; it continually advances the science of sales and the art of the customer relationship; it experiments to refine best practices — and innovate new ones — in satisfying customer needs; and it vouches for and demonstrates the firm's commitment to look beyond its own financial goals and fulfill a larger mission, a noble purpose.

First and foremost, making a sales organization great begins with great leadership. Effective sales leaders regularly get out into the field to observe, inspect, teach, coach, and sell. These behaviors ensure that they are never blinded by the numbers but always understand their human impact and their true significance in terms of customer behavior and the sales organization's performance.

Recognizing that command-and-control leadership practices are outmoded, today's best sales executives lead by example and in collaboration with both salespeople and customers. They empower salespeople to take the initiative in creating and delivering value for customers. They earn the status of trusted business partners in customers' eyes, and they enlist customers in product and service development. They lead by listening, striving to learn all they can from both their salespeople and their customers about where the market is going and what will make the essential difference in meeting customer needs.

Within a firm, the customer-motivated sales organization as a whole performs a similar leadership function, identifying customer needs and interacting with other business functions to develop and deliver customer value. Sales executives and the sales organization are a firm's advance guard in entering areas of market complexity and risk and winning differential advantage over the competition.

Second, customer-motivated sales organizations display their commitment to a larger mission and leading from the front in their human resource practices. With no lack of toughness when called for, they build a culture that nurtures and inspires excellence. In this context, sales leaders manage their people by activity, not short-term results, as the best way to achieve great long-term performance. They align highly motivating reward and recognition programs with customer needs through clear expectations and transparent measurement.

Third, the complex challenges and brutal competitiveness of today's business environment require that sales organizations continually hone and increase their intellectual capital. Customer-motivated sales organizations are the ones best positioned to advance the science of sales and the art of the customer relationship. They anticipate and meet changing customer needs with ever more precise resource allocation across multiple customer segments and sales channels, continuous improvement and innovation of sales processes and sales operations, and sales roles that may evolve in generalist and specialist dimensions. Through increasingly sophisticated sales analytics, they acquire and exploit customer understanding at a fundamental level.

Fourth, customer-motivated sales organizations are change-friendly. They shun complacency and consider all existing best practices provisional, subject to replacement whenever they find, invent, or recognize even better practices. To this end they continually experiment as organizations, and they foster creative risk-taking and experimentation by their people. Understanding that success only comes through trial and error, they empower salespeople to fail and celebrate learning from mistakes, so long as this occurs in the course of a genuine effort to create and deliver customer value. The only limit they enforce is on repeating mistakes. By encouraging "loud" mistakes that are quickly recognized, they follow a "fail or scale" approach that is cost-effective and highly productive.

The fifth, culminating characteristic is that customer-motivated sales organizations live their missions. Remember, living the mission has a business purpose. It is not altruism, but the best way of creating win–win interactions between a firm and its customers. When a sales organization lives a larger mission than quarterly revenue and profit goals, it builds credibility and trust with customers and secures differential advantage over competitors. Living the mission aligns a firm's resources with customer needs. It attracts the best talent and accelerates its training and performance. This talent acquisition applies to both the rank-and-file members of a sales organization and its leadership, for as one sales executive memorably told us, "You can't inspire unless you're inspired." Last, but not least, a focus on a larger mission prevents complacency and keeps a sales organization alert to changes in customer behavior and customer needs.

* * *

We believe these five linked activities represent a crucial new model for sales organizations: *Sales-added value.*

## *Sales-Added Value*

Early in the life cycle of a new product or service, when a firm offers greater benefits and value than competing alternatives, the sales job is often relatively straightforward. Quite simply, the sales force has to deliver the superiority message and let buyers make informed decisions.

But as product and service categories mature, even firms with the greatest R&D investments tend to lose a decisive edge in functional benefits. Human capital and technological know-how shift from firm to firm, and competitors whittle away at the original market leader's once attractive, functional-benefit-driven profit margins.

In the increasingly competitive environment that virtually all companies face today, how should the firm counteract the inexorable pressure to commoditization as aggressive competitors erase product-and-service differentiation benefits and cut prices? The answer, we believe, is via sales-added value. The firms that we profile in this book are living exemplars of this new paradigm.

Such companies:

- Invest in understanding the key business issues faced by their key clients/industries served.

- Invest in segmenting their markets to identify groups of customers whose bottom line can be meaningfully impacted by their products and services.

- Invest in creating new products/applications/processes that can be sold and delivered by their sales and related customer-facing assets.

- Prepare their customer-facing assets to find such opportunities at their customers, calculate the ROI of doing business with them, and sell high to executives that care about bottom-line impact.

Why do companies choose a sales-value-add strategy if it takes so much investment? It's the one form of differentiation that you control. It's not dependent on products or technology, at least not exclusively. Differentiation in the sales-added value model depends primarily on a deep understanding of customer business issues. The benefits of this kind of differentiation include:

- Value that is hard to replicate; the value that a seller brings cannot be reverse engineered.

- Growth plans are not held hostage to the killer app that never arrives.

- Improved growth and margins in a meaningful slice of the business.

- Freedom to innovate in lower cost channels and sales strategies among accounts that want only the lowest price alternative.

What characterizes companies that succeed in a sales-value-add strategy?

- They have strong, interactive relationships with their marketing departments that help develop and deploy applications and services that are both implementable and highly valued by customers; marketing teams interface with sales to gather insights into what is valued and how to deliver it.

- They have strong development programs that produce the kind of sellers capable of bringing ROI-type messages to high level, C-suite buyers; the strong relationship with marketing produces tools and cases that help demonstrate the ROI impact.

- They have access to the data, cases, tools, and specialists needed to design and implement the solutions that they have described and sold; they make the investments needed to deliver, rather than try to get by with a "some assembly required" type of sale, which can kill a value sales initiative before it even gets started.

We found plentiful evidence of this strategic thrust when we checked back with sales organizations to see what impact the Great Recession had on them. Our follow-up interviews showed that the highest performing sales organizations continue to focus rigorously on the five linked activities of leading from the front, speaking softly — and carrying a big carrot, refining the science of sales and the art of the customer relationship, making loud mistakes, and living the mission. The executives we spoke to credited the intellectual, ethical, and relationship capital that these five activities produce with helping them to come through the recession stronger than when it began.

Michael Orrick of Thomson Reuters Legal was one of several sales executives to describe the downturn triggered by the credit crisis as remarkable not only for its depth and duration but also for its impact on the pace of technological and market change. Orrick said:

> *Coming out of the recession, my take is this: A properly skilled sales organization unlocks the voice of the customer in a completely different way. A great sales organization brings back such a rich seam of customer information, and that is critical right now because of the accelerated pace of change.*

Orrick and his sales organization engage customers in a three-phase process of "enriching our offerings for them." He explained:

> *The first phase of the sales organization adding value for customers is knocking out the speed bumps, smoothing out what is not right. What would they like to change today? What would make this product immediately more valuable to the way they work?*

*The second phase is involving the customer in setting product priorities for the next one to two years. What are the key leverage points for their business over that time?*

*If you can do one and two successfully, and only deep sales and account management people who live very close to the customer can do this, you can then play the third card. You can actually engage a customer, and groups of customers, in a true partnering on long-term strategy.*

*What I like to be able to get to with significant customer groups is that five-year picture of where their whole industry is going and what we can bring to help them through that change. Then you can add product leadership together with thought leadership.*

*That goes beyond product and domain expertise. It goes much wider than a set of products. It goes into the empty spaces where there are no products yet.*

Similarly, Mike Fasulo, executive vice president and chief marketing officer at Sony Electronics, observed that the sales organization "is the tip of the spear and its biggest value is in living the brand and building a long-term relationship with customers through continuity, commitment, and sustainability." This role naturally falls to salespeople, Fasulo said, because they "are the best at understanding and translating in both directions, from the customer to the company and from the company to the customer."

One winning example of delivering two-sided wins during the recession that Fasulo shared with us occurred at Costco. As we had earlier discussed with Mike Fasulo's colleague Ken Stevens, one of the big challenges for the Sony Electronics sales organization are unassisted retail selling floors, where customers are on their own. Fasulo recounted:

*Costco is an unassisted floor. It is a treasure hunt. Yet at Sony we pride ourselves on being a premium company with quality products at a premium price. How do you do that on an unassisted floor in a discount price club, where products sit on pallets in a virtual warehouse?*

*We have a notion inside Sony called Sony United. It means working across Sony Pictures, Sony Music, Sony Electronics, Sony Computer*

*Entertainment to represent one brand Sony. The tough question is, how do you translate that in the retail environment?*

*In this case with Costco, the sales representatives calling on Costco came forward with an idea of differentiating Sony from the pack by putting a variety of products together in one very compelling experience on a Costco pallet. They asked themselves this question: If we bundled television, Blu-ray player, and associated content, was there a value bundle we could provide the Costco membership customer that would not be in conflict with how we go to market in the general marketplace, while stimulating consumers to buy through showing them an integrated home theater experience from Sony?*

*They did it. The salespeople came up with an eye-catching solution that clearly delineates Sony from anybody else, and that adds value for both Costco and Sony. You might not think a display on a sales floor would have such an impact, but the CEOs of Costco and Sony Electronics connected to talk about it, because it was breaking new ground and meeting a need on both sides that was not met previously.*

Referring to the recession, Fasulo emphasized how high-performing sales organizations "shelter and protect their companies" through tough times. One of the hallmarks of Sony and the other high-performing sales organizations profiled in this book was continuing investment in their people during the downturn. For example, Kevin Warren, president of Xerox's U.S. Solutions Group, said:

*We had to weather the storm, and to do that we leveraged the institutional knowledge of the turnaround years in the early 2000s in an amazing way. But we also wanted to strengthen our competitive position, so we still kept a focus on the salespeople. We still hired. We still trained. We still kept our incentives like president's clubs. A lot of our competitors cut.*

*That really helped us from a share position. As the economy slowly turns around, we are in a lot stronger position than when we entered the recession.*

Warren pointed out that in the global economy, technological innovation rarely lasts for more than a six-to-nine-month window. "The way to separate yourself and get out of the commodity trap is when your salespeople really understand customers' business challenges and can add value to their businesses." That puts an enormous premium on the sales organization's intellectual capital and on enhancing it with "business acumen training in ROI from the customer's perspective."

Warren concluded, "That is not an easy thing to build in a sales organization, but it is a powerful competitive advantage." His peers at other high-performing sales organizations sounded the same theme when we spoke to them about the impact of the recession.

Looking across Cisco's global sales efforts, Rob Lloyd, executive vice president for worldwide operations, said that the sales organization's intellectual capital "has created a business agility to address the recession, help our partners and customers to get through it, and continue to enter new markets." George O'Meara, Cisco's senior vice president for the U.S. and Canadian theater, added, "When our salespeople talk to customers, it is not a technology discussion anymore. It is a business discussion."

The need to engage customers in terms of their business challenges predates the recession, of course. But the downturn has made it all the more true that, as Matt Mills, Oracle's senior vice president for North American applications sales, put it, "You can no longer grow your business transactionally." Hence it is essential to have "sales reps who are smart about industry solutions and our customers' business problems. Solving those relevant business problems can drive higher value for customers and in doing so drive higher value for the sales organization."

Mills added:

> *A customer's problems never match up exactly with a piece of software. We take the best of the best, and put it together for the customer using our enabling technology. Those solution sets deliver four to five times more revenue than a typical sale in the transactional model.*

Speaking to the same point in terms of all of Oracle's North American sales efforts, Keith Block said:

> *The economic meltdown made being a trusted advisor and helping our customers navigate troubled waters even more important. When most of the competition was cutting, we continued to inno-*

*vate and provide customers with a tremendous amount of resources and brainpower — at our own expense.*

*That's a fundamental key to our success: We never stop investing in the customer. We never stop investing in ourselves, either.*

*Again, while others were cutting, we continued to invest in initiatives like sales leadership training to foster a culture of leadership at all levels. We continued to stress doing the right thing and leading by example, leading from the front.*

*Through our customer-first focus and our best-of-breed acquisition strategy, we've achieved something that has been a dream in the industry for a decade: Truly end-to-end software, hardware, and services.*

*Exceptional salespeople, an exceptional culture, and an exceptional portfolio combine to form a perfect storm. As our competition faltered in the recession, we grew stronger and closer to our customers. The quality and integrity of the sales organization coupled with world-class solutions enabled us to offer customers the ability to invest in solutions with immediate return and impact so they could succeed in the downturn and create separation from their competitors. By continuing to drive unprecedented success to our customers, we will in turn continue to increase separation from our competitors.*

As we've said more than once, the Oracle sales organization's distinctive style is obviously part and parcel of its sales effectiveness. But what interests us even more is what the Oracle sales organization has in common with other high-performing sales organizations. Every great sales organization has its own personality, but they all focus intensely on delivering increasing value to customers through ever-increasing intellectual capital and business acumen.

For example, Bruce Dahlgren, senior vice president for worldwide enterprise sales in HP's imaging and printing group, shared insights with us on how many companies respond to tough times by concentrating on their product and service sets. Yet, Dahlgren said, "[T]hey do not spend equal energy on making sure that the sales force transforms with the products, and has the preparation, skill, and support to sell them."

This is hardly a recipe for success. The sales force, its support structures, and its interaction with marketing must all change in a unified way to respond to changing market conditions and to execute new sales models. Indeed, Dahlgren asserted in language that was echoed at other high-performing sales organizations, "You cannot just go out and hire and train a talented sales force, and then not shift your marketing efforts and sales operations to support them."

But when a company does activate those levers in a unified way with effective product offerings, its addressable market and potential share of wallet expand both within existing customer segments and adjacent areas. A critical aspect of this evolution in high-tech markets is that the sales organization must sell to both end users and decision makers in customer organizations, "up to and including the CIO, CFO, and even the CEO."

Dahlgren said wryly:

> *I often tell the sales force that the sale really starts when you introduce new concepts and the customer says no. You move to a value-add solution when you get the customer to do something they had not already planned. If the customer was already going to say yes, why would you need a sales force?*
>
> *When you can say you have a consultative sales force is when the customer would almost pay you to sell to them — when instead of chasing demand, you are introducing new concepts, demonstrating new value, and creating new demand.*
>
> *Again, that requires cross-functional change in sales and marketing. Instead of general, broad-stroke marketing programs, the marketing team has to map into the sales process and do consultative marketing to support the sales team's consultative selling.*
>
> *That is how you both support the core and find future growth areas. And it is very exciting to go out and generate this type of demand in existing and new accounts by adding solutions and value.*

\* \* \*

Our final example of growing through the downturn, thanks to sales-added value, comes from Cisco. Cisco's product portfolio has expanded over the years from core networking technologies to major new categories in adjacent market spaces. Such product expansion has posed challenges for Cisco's direct sales organization, its many channel partners, and its customers.

Rob Lloyd said:

> *We were a bit siloed. Our technology story did not always feel completely aligned, and the service strategy did not always feel aligned with the product strategy.*

To address this issue, Lloyd sponsored a pilot program called Cisco 3.0. The first thing Cisco 3.0 did right was that it had buy-in from senior management, including CEO John Chambers and the board of directors. In Lloyd's words:

> *Cisco 3.0 was regularly reviewed at the senior executive level and by our board of directors. So it had a lot of visibility. The objective of the program was to transform relationships with our top 30 global customers, and the experience we were delivering to them, by simplifying how we do business and establishing channels for deeper and more frequent interaction.*

> *Through Cisco 3.0, we received feedback from our customers that they wanted an easier and more consistent global sales experience and that they wanted a single point of contact. One of the biggest changes we made in the sales organization was the creation of a client director role for our Cisco 3.0 accounts. We completely consolidated all of our resources around the world behind these client directors, and empowered them to lead the transformation in each of their accounts.*

The Cisco 3.0 pilot program eventually evolved into a broader initiative called "One Cisco," that Lloyd explained is focused on driving cross-functional collaboration, alignment, and investment across every function in the company. "Operating as One Cisco will ultimately enable us to deliver a faster, easier, and more seamless experience to our customers and partners around the world."

To support this effort, Cisco deployed its telepresence technology and "enterprise class social networking tools" inside the top 30 global accounts. It put cross-functional teams against an array of customer issues, a development we've already looked at in chapter 1, "Lead from the Front." And it also leveraged its channel partners, an area where Cisco has few, if any, equals in our view. Rob Lloyd told us, "We like the feeling that every day there are 250,000 people outside our organization who make their living selling Cisco products, and we really do think of them and train them as a seamless extension of our sales force."

Speaking to this point, Wendy Bahr, Cisco's senior vice president for global and transformational partnerships, noted that in many cases outside the largest customers, the Cisco partner will lead the sales effort and the Cisco direct sales organization "will play a supportive role." This process flows, Bahr said, from CEO John Chambers' early decision that Cisco and its outside sellers should "try to partner for life. Many other companies have a volume model with their channel partners. We pride ourselves on having a value model."

Bahr continued:

> We are continually pushing the envelope on new technology, and we are coupling that with channel partners who can provide solutions to customers in a consultative way.
>
> Our partners stand by us because we stand by them. Through the downturn we continued to provide programs, support, and incentives so that they could come out of the downturn stronger than ever before. And that has really helped us to slingshot around the downturn to come out even better and stronger.

In terms of Cisco 3.0's development and execution of One Cisco for customers, the channel partners vastly amplify the resources that client directors and account executives can deploy. George O'Meara said, "The client directors and account executives have at their disposal not only the skill sets available throughout Cisco but also those that are appropriate from partners."

The most far-reaching aspect of One Cisco was shaking off the last vestiges of Cisco's prior sales model, which George O'Meara described as "very transactional." To make its vastly expanded product portfolio pay off, Cisco had to achieve a consultative relationship with customers and "build a competitive base around sales." This in turn meant moving to what Rob Lloyd described as selling not just solutions but entire architectures for data centers and similar scale projects.

Lloyd explained that, like any large-scale change effort, the Cisco 3.0 initiative had to overcome the uncertainty and reservations of many within the organization, especially since "we made these changes in the midst of the economic downturn." But the impact of Cisco 3.0 on Cisco's top 30 global customers "was that these very large accounts actually became our fastest growing."

When we spoke to Rob Lloyd and his colleagues about Cisco 3.0, they were focused on rolling it out to another 500 accounts, those Cisco considered "transformational, not only because they are big or have big potential but because they are really trying to transform their business." This effort involved bringing together communities of client directors and account executives across both Cisco and its partner network in order to share best practices. Cisco's aggressive plans will require immense managerial energy and talent, especially in the next phase when, Lloyd said, Cisco will be "scaling what we learned from Cisco 3.0 to the next 5,000 accounts."

For the individual sales person, either in Cisco's direct sales force or in one of its channel partners, Lloyd described a future of "participating in social communities of salespeople that share winning strategies across the entire Cisco ecosystem." The big challenge for salespeople, as for the sales organization as a whole, will be continually improving their expertise and intellectual capital and executing with speed and agility. "Those who embrace this challenge," Lloyd asserted, "using social networking and collaboration technologies to build deeper relationships, share best practices, and access information and expertise, will move quickly to be winners and top performers."

\* \* \*

## *Conclusion*

Based on the evidence we have gathered from top sales organizations, we would generalize Rob Lloyd's observation to sellers and sales organizations throughout the 21st-century business landscape.

Excellence in five areas — leading from the front, building a customer-motivated culture by speaking clearly and carrying a big carrot, advancing the science of sales and the art of the customer relationship, making loud mistakes, and living the mission — characterizes the most consistently successful sales organizations in every sector of the B2B world. As we've seen, top performers as disparate as Cisco, FedEx, Genzyme, Honeywell, Hewlett-Packard, Johnson & Johnson and its Vistakon subsidiary, Johnson Controls, MasterCard, Oracle, Pitney Bowes, Sony Electronics, Thomson Reuters

Legal, Whirlpool, and Xerox all share these characteristics and base their long-term market leadership on them.

To join these companies at the top it is not enough to emulate one or two of these characteristics. Successful organizations do them ALL well. You can, too, and if you want to grow, you may have little choice.

These are the companies where top sellers can be heroes. Where sales executives have a shot at the top job. Where sales is viewed as the co-equal of marketing and finance in the hunt for growth and profit. Where an investment in sales infrastructure is viewed as an investment in the future. These companies are customer-motivated and proud of it. They know that nothing happens until the sale is made. They know that customer satisfaction and loyalty flow from the value that great sales organizations add as much or more than from the products and services a company develops. They know that sales is the linchpin between marketing's understanding of customer needs and finance's understanding of the profit equation. Customer motivation, the ability to leverage sales to package and deliver value at a profit, is what sets these companies apart.

It is no coincidence, we believe, that these firms have responded well to the most difficult economic conditions in decades. Their resilience since the subprime mortgage bubble burst and triggered a wider credit crisis exemplifies the core, multifaceted business role that the modern sales organization must play and the substantial intellectual capital it requires to out-think, out-offer, and out-perform the competition.

# APPENDIX 1
# Interviewees and Titles

**THE FOLLOWING IS A LIST OF INTERVIEWEES** identified by company and organizational position at the time of the most recent interview.

Sam Abdelnour — Vice President, U.S. Sales, Whirlpool Corporation

Wendy Bahr — Senior Vice President, US and Canada Partner Organization, Cisco, Inc.

Keith Block — Executive Vice President, North America Sales, Oracle Corporation

Ron Boire — President, Toys "R" Us, North America, Toys "R" Us, Inc.

Joe Brennan — Vice President, Sales, Genzyme Corporation

Jay Connor — Vice President, Global Sales Support, Hewlett-Packard Company

Bruce Dahlgren — Senior Vice President, Global Enterprise Business, Imaging and Printing Group, Hewlett-Packard Company

Dave Edmonds — Senior Vice President, Worldwide Services, FedEx Corporation

Mike Fasulo — Executive Vice President and Chief Marketing Officer, Sony Electronics, Inc.

James Firestone — President, Xerox North America, Xerox Corporation

Gary Flood — Executive Vice President, Global Account Management, MasterCard Worldwide

Rob Fruithandler — Vice President, Channel Management, Pitney Bowes, Inc.

Valarie Gelb — Chief Global Sales Development Officer, MasterCard Worldwide

Olivier Kohler — Senior Vice President and General Manager, Enterprise Strategic Alliances, Hewlett-Packard Company

Rob Lloyd — Executive Vice President, Worldwide Operations, Cisco, Inc.

Gregory Lorden — Senior Vice President and General Manager Americas, Business Objects Corporation

Michael MacDonald — President, Global Accounts and Marketing Operations, Xerox Corporation

Kevin Madden — Vice President, Global Sales, Honeywell Building Solutions, Honeywell International, Inc.

Jeff Marshall — Vice President, Customer Marketing, Pitney Bowes, Inc.

Andy Mattes — Senior Vice President and Chief Sales Officer, Technology Solutions Group, Hewlett-Packard Company

Kim Metcalf-Kupres — Vice President, Global Sales and Marketing, Johnson Controls, Inc.

Matt Mills — Senior Vice President, North America Strategic Accounts, Application Sales, Oracle Corporation

George O'Meara — Senior Vice President, Customer Advocacy U.S. and Canada, Cisco, Inc.

Michael Orrick — Vice President, Large Law Sales & Account Management, Thomson Reuters Corporation

Sue Petrella — Vice President, Corporate Accounts, Johnson & Johnson Health Care Systems, Inc.

David Provost — Director, Sales, Whirlpool Corporation

Daniel Regan — Senior Vice President, US Renal Business, Genzyme Corporation

Thomas Schmitt — Senior Vice President, FedEx Solutions, FedEx Corporation

David Smith — Vice President, Sales, Vistakon, Inc.

Ken Stevens —  Senior Vice President, National Sales, Sony Electronics, Inc.

Jay Vandenbree — President, Consumer Sales, Sony Electronics, Inc.

Kevin Warren — President, U.S. Solutions Group, Xerox Corporation

# APPENDIX 2
# Selecting the Top Customer-Motivated Sales Organizations

**THE COMPANIES STUDIED IN THIS BOOK** were selected by a two-step process.

First, we identified industries where selling counts. We excluded industries where sales are driven largely by brand advertising (consumer) and/or promotion intensity (pharmaceuticals, insurance). We were most interested in examining industries in which sellers play a central role in explaining product/service functions and applying products and services to solving business problems for their customers. The industries (and companies) we identified turned out to be predominantly, but not exclusively, B2B, where product options are complex and where sales processes have multiple steps. Our assumption was that in such situations sales-coverage excellence would spell the difference between average and outstanding results. These industries included:

- **Application and systems software:** Sellers are central to delivering insight into software functionality. At the highest levels of achievement, sellers deliver insight into how software can be used to improve both customer business processes and firm profitability.

- **Consumer appliances:** Sellers deliver insight and value to retail distribution partners by offering insight into: a) how to more effectively merchandize products in highly competitive markets, and b) how to manage order volumes to optimize retail inventory levels.

- **Computers and office equipment:** Sellers at minimum deliver information and insight on product functionality. At their best, sellers deliver business process improvement programs to help their customers operate more efficiently and effectively.

- **Credit cards:** Sellers work with client banks to design and deliver cutting-edge credit services that help merchants better target and service customers.

- **Mail and transportation:** Sellers work with customers to refine and optimize supply chain logistics, leading to both lower costs and enhanced services.

- **Medical products:** Sales professionals consult with healthcare providers about product usage and office administration on how to more efficiently manage costs/inventories for improved operating efficiency.

- **Biotechnology:** Highly skilled sellers take complex products to market, offering physicians insights on how to use these compounds to achieve improved patient outcomes.

- **Networking equipment:** Sellers deliver complex systems of hardware and software configured to help customers run optimized voice and data communications networks.

Second, for each relevant industry category we looked at 10 years of performance, 1999 through 2009. These years included two tough recessions when selling excellence truly separated the best from the rest. For this 10-year period, we examined three performance dimensions:

- **Overall growth:** What was the 10-year compound annual growth rate (CAGR)?

- **Consistency:** In how many years during the 10-year period was a company's revenue growth "best in class"?

- **Profitability:** In how many years (if any) did the company lose money?

We sought companies that a) were tops in 10-year compound **organic** growth (no credit for M&A), b) achieved consistent growth (were near the top of the growth chart every year, including recession years), and c) consistently made money.

Listed in the following table are the companies that emerged from this analysis along with a summary of their 10-year performance.

| Industry | Company | 10-Year Organic CAGR | 10-Year Organic CAGR Rank | Years in 75th Percentile of Organic Growth | Profitable Years |
|---|---|---|---|---|---|
| Application Software | Business Objects* | 30.8%* | 1* | 6/8* | 8/8 |
| System Software | Oracle | 8.6% | 4 | 6/11 | 11/11 |
| Consumer Appliances | Whirlpool | 5.0% | 1 | 7/11 | 10/11 |
| Computers and Office Equipment | HP | 10.5% | 1 | 8/11 | 10/11 |
| Credit Cards | MasterCard | 18.5% | 1 | 5/9** | 7/9 |
| Mail and Transport | FedEx | 6.9% | 1 | 7/11 | 11/11 |
| Pharma and Medical Products | J&J | 8.3% | 2 | 7/11 | 11/11 |
| Bio-tech | Genzyme | 21.8% | 2 | 7/11 | 7/11 |
| Telecom Equipment | Cisco | 11.5% | 1 | 6/11 | 10/11 |

*Business Objects acquired by SAP in fourth quarter, 2007; metrics only accumulated from 1999 to 2006.

**Numbers unavailable prior to 2001

Along with the companies identified above, we examined several others: Honeywell, Johnson Controls, Pitney Bowes, Sony, Thomson Reuters, Toys "R" Us, and Xerox.

- **Honeywell.** At Honeywell we specifically focused on Honeywell Building Solutions, part of Honeywell's historic core. This division has delivered first-order growth results since 2003 after a "near-death" experience in 2002. This turnaround performance was, we believed, well worth examining.

- **Johnson Controls.** This is a first-rate company across all of its core businesses, and is far and away the number one provider of Power Solutions in North America. We explored this division.

- **Pitney Bowes.** A quiet performer in the office equipment space, Pitney Bowes has consistently dominated mail metering, and has demonstrated an ability to parlay that dominance into adjacent growth opportunities.

- **Sony.** Sony's continuing dominance as an iconic consumer electronics brand, despite increasing competition from fierce rivals, cannot be denied. We wanted to find out how its sales organization operated behind the scenes in this company better known for product excellence.

- **Thomson Reuters.** This firm has a dominant position in data services for both the financial and legal sectors. It used the recent recession as an opportunity to up its game, take share and build loyalty. We examined Thomson Reuters Legal.

- **Toys "R" Us.** The president of U.S. Toys "R" Us at the time of our interviews, Ron Boire (now Brookstone CEO), was formerly a top executive at Sony Electronics, where he pioneered strategies to partner with the distribution channel. He offered keen insights on how sellers can add value to the buy/sell equation.

- **Xerox.** Xerox is another iconic brand which can lay claim to both a huge and successful recent turnaround as well as high-end performance in the competitive Computers and Office Equipment area.

The observations and conclusions in this book derive from secondary research into each of these organizations, and in-depth personal interviews with key executives in sales, sales operations, and marketing. We set out to better understand the operations, character, and composition of sales organizations that deliver exceptional results year after year. In our interviews with these executives we inquired about what mattered most to them in the following areas:

- **Culture:** What types of results and behaviors are really valued at your company? What type of seller do you try to attract? Who are your sales heroes?

- **Innovation:** What value do you deliver that really separates you from the competition? Where did the ideas for value come from?

- **Internal relationships:** How do sales, sales operations, and marketing work together? How do top sales executives face off with other functions?

- **Leadership practices:** How do sales leaders capture the hearts and minds of sellers? What is the role of the sales leader in building a "customer-motivated" sales organization?

- **Organization:** What types of sales resources do you deploy to face off against the competition and deliver value to customers?

- **Planning practices:** What role does the sales function play in the planning process? Where does the top sales executive sit among other functional heads in the firm's planning process?

- **Product:** What messages do you stress to your customers; what sets you apart? Is it the products you sell or is it the way sellers package products and services into something of higher value?

Out of the interviews we distilled the characteristics of greatness common to all these organizations and identified the cases that best illustrated how these companies nurture a customer-motivated culture that delivers exceptional value and superior results year after year.